The Colour Guide
to
Crystal Healing

J . S . STUART

quantum
LONDON ● NEW YORK ● TORONTO ● SYDNEY

quantum

An imprint of W. Foulsham & Co. Ltd.,
The Publishing House, Bennetts Close,
Cippenham, Berkshire SL1 5AP, England.

ISBN 0-572-02257-3
Copyright © 1996 W. Foulsham & Co. Ltd.
Crystals supplied by The Rock Warehouse, Ilford, Essex.

Typeset by Brains Typography, Reading.
Printed in Great Britain by St. Edmundsbury Press, Bury St. Edmunds, Suffolk.

Contents

Introduction

*T*HROUGHOUT the four dimensions of the universe, with which our lives are irrevocably entwined, is a known constant: energy cannot be created or destroyed.

Matter may be transformed into energy and energy into matter. Matter is built with energy and from energy, and contains energy.

Hence, under a primitive sun millions of years ago, when giant horsetails and other swamp plants grew with the power of the sun, harvesting the energy from the skies along with nutrients and stability from the young Earth, the plants built their cells million upon million, billion upon billion. The energy of the sun had been gathered – the energy was still there, but in a different form. It hadn't been destroyed – it had been used and transformed into matter, in this case the stuff of cells and food to power the plant.

As plants naturally die and decompose, they disperse the matter in the form of food for other creatures, which use it as an energy source. However, millions of years ago in the geological time known as the carboniferous era, many plants did not naturally decompose. The trees and horsetails had lived in swampy conditions, and when they died they sank beneath the oxygen-poor waters to the muds below and were cut off from the oxygen supply needed by micro-organisms and fungi to digest aerobically the fallen plants. These plants accumulated over the ages, their water forced out by the pressures of further additions, and then by mineral sedimentation on top of that, so that the plants were crushed together. These are the coal seams so efficiently exploited since the Industrial Revolution of the nineteenth century.

Coal powered the Industrial Revolution – coal that once was plant life that harnessed and used energy from the sun. When coal burns, in a sense the result is a release of all the gathered energy from a primitive sky. Coal can therefore be seen as a storer of energy – an exhaustible

5

store somewhat like a battery; the power of the sun, crushed and fashioned by the depths of the Earth.

Many rocks are like this. The powers they hold have been derived from the air (from the wind and sun), from the Earth (from those deep pressures within the body of the Earth), from fire (from the heat of molten rock, dramatic as it bursts upon the surface of the Earth), and from water (from the darkness of the ocean we know so little about); from the energies all around. The process is a continuous one.

Energy cannot be created or destroyed, but it can be captured, and in some instances successfully. If energy can be captured by coal and put to a useful purpose, why then should this be an isolated instance? Perhaps there are other examples. Look carefully.

For thousands of years people have known this to be so. People all across the world in a common subconsciousness have gathered stones for specific purposes, as batteries for energy, as releasers of their own energy, as healers. Should such accumulated knowledge from thousands of years of experience be dismissed out of hand? How arrogantly we modern-day people exist within our protective sphere. Ours is the arrogance of ignorance. When stripped of our technological protection we are as frightened children. I am reminded of an old Chinese proverb, which states 'One must become like a child if one is to learn'.

Energy cannot be created or destroyed – but it can be harnessed. A century ago scientists would have been laughed at if they'd suggested that power could be created from fusing hydrogen atoms, and yet now even children know this. There is energy all around us. All we need to do is close our eyes and … feel.

When you next switch on an electric light, think of the electricity, where it comes from and what the power source is. It may come from coal, gas, oil, nuclear, hydro or even wind power; there is energy all around us, which exists – with us or without us.

The world is full of wonder. There is no doubt the world is more than we can see. Our eyes are sensitive only to the visible part of the spectrum, our ears do not hear beyond a limited range. Increasingly we are beginning to see ourselves not as part of the world but apart from the world. This can blind us to the world's wonders. And ours is only one small part of a vast universe.

The continents of our world, these oases of life amid the dark void, are areas of rock almost floating upon the semi-fluid lithosphere beneath. Upon these continents billions of us exist. Beneath them are the hot regions of the Earth's interior, churning the convection currents of the mantle to move the continents above. Although the timescale is far greater than our limited lifetimes, our world is in a state of constant flux. New rocks are constantly being created from the recycled materials of destroyed older ones. We stand on rock, we build from rock, and in our glasshouses we throw rocks.

But how much do we really know? We may think we are masters of technology, but we are really just on the edge of a greater knowledge.

We know, for instance, that it would take several million years for the heat energy generated from a small piece of granite (from the captured radionuclides) to boil a cup of water. We know about the chemical make-up of minerals as we gaze down our microscopes, and yet people are made up of many of the same constituents, albeit in different quantities. We also know how precious gold is – people have killed and died for gold; they have spent their energies hoarding it.

Is that really all we know and want to know? As a people we are fascinated by mystery, but we need not be afraid. There is never any need to be afraid. Science teaches that the Earth was created from an accretion of dust material, drawn in by increasingly powerful gravitational forces as the sun was being created. What powerful energies these are. Energy cannot be created or destroyed. We continue to orbit the sun at 1,000 mph, plunging into the darkness and coldness of an unknown, and all we really are is a tiny planet in a vast universe, the scale of which is completely incomprehensible.

We know from volcanoes and earthquakes that the energies inside the Earth continue to be powerful and destructive. In time the continents we know today will be changed beyond recognition by an energy we can hardly comprehend; the same energy that moves continents or spins the world. As in all matters, energy need not be destructive if it can be harnessed. We live in a world full of minerals, created by great energies, and yet dare we explore further than we can see?

We all know there is more to life than we can see. We feel it in the deepest night, we glimpse it in tales of long ago. We are only human and it is human to be curious. Through us streams the past on its way to the future, and most of the time we are unaware.

CHAPTER ONE

Crystals, Minerals and Precious Stones

THE most common question asked is what do crystals actually do? Crystals can change your life. They have the ability to bring out the best in a person. They can reach deep to enhance your strengths for a better quality of life. This is all about energy and the search for something more fitting for the individual. Everyone is different, with different strengths and weaknesses. Each person must be seen as an individual – there are different crystals for different people who have the will to use them.

Since before the very first word was written people have valued crystals, minerals and precious stones, sometimes worshipped them. The commercial value of ores and gems is undoubted, the beauty of some of them made eternal by poets and lovers. Throughout history precious metals and stones have been lasting symbols of status. This is part of the culture upon which our civilisation has been based.

However beautiful, valuable and powerful such materials are, how many people through the ages have wondered about the mechanisms of production and growth of these materials?

Take a simple matchstick. When you hold it in your hand do you see the sun shining through the years of growth of the wood, the seasons changing the snow to sun again? Can you feel the tree's roots delve and grip the Earth, the transpiration from outstretched fingered branches drawing up water-soluble nutrients?

Although it has been produced by different mechanisms, a stone, a gem, a crystal, is no different. It has been produced by energy, and a measure of the energy remains. How can we know this? We can feel.

Many people think of outer space as a cold, dark void – almost a nothingness. Relative to the Earth's abundance this may be true, yet everything is relative, and in reality and scientifically, space is far from being a void. In space, for example, lingering background radiation holds the temperature slightly above absolute zero. The rise in temperature above absolute zero is only slight, and yet it is there and is detectable with intricate instrumentation. Without such instrumentation we would not know.

Thus, simply because we cannot directly feel something doesn't mean it fails to exist. It would be pure arrogance to state any differently. Of course, there are matters our senses cannot perceive. We cannot see far ultra-violet or deep infra-red, yet they exist. We cannot detect the energy from stones because we don't know what we're looking for, and it is likely to be masked by the surrounding environment – by sunshine, noise, even the Earth's magnetic field.

Let's take the Earth's magnetic field as an example. We know the gravitational pull of the moon has a distinct effect on the world we know. The magnetic effect of our own world retains many unknowns; how does it affect us? It affects iron, so does it affect the iron in us? Does it affect the iron minerals of use in crystal healing? Logic would suggest it does. We readily accept the effects of the moon's gravitational field, but ignore the effects of our own world's magnetic field. Any effects from the latter will be subtle, but crystal healing works by subtlety. It may be no accident that some of the most energetic minerals within the realm of crystal healing are iron-bearing minerals. This may be because they draw energy directly from the Earth's magnetic field. No one has conducted research into this, no one has measured or analysed it, so to many it simply doesn't exist. The only research being conducted which may be associated with this is the highly secret work into zero-point energy – energy that should not exist. Once ridiculed by conventional science, zero-point energy is now being researched by notable groups eager to tap into this mysterious energy source.

Stones, minerals and especially crystals maintain fragile remnants of their original building energy. The colour is important, as is the way you hold them and the way you concentrate to feel the subtle energy. The energy available can so easily be lost, in the same way that sound can be blocked out by closing a window or door. Your door must be

9

open for you to be receptive to the energy potential. In some instances the energy level will be so far beyond our meagre senses – either higher or lower – it will only work subconsciously. Yet it will work, if you allow it to work, if you want it to work. The colour of the mineral or crystal usually works in this way. Different colours usually denote different energy levels, many of which will be out of range of our senses.

Since before the very first word was written people have valued crystals, minerals and precious stones. This has been mainly for their commercial value and their beauty, with few daring to admit to anything else because there has always been a difficulty in understanding. However, all through the ages such materials have also been cherished for reasons more powerful than wealth. Crystal healing is not a new phenomenon.

Much like a tree, the roots of crystal healing delve deep and connect with hidden history. Perhaps the ancients knew more than we do – very little was written down, so who can say? What we can say with certainty, however, is that crystal healing has never been so popular. So many people can't all be wrong.

CHAPTER TWO

How to Use Crystals

❖

E ACH crystal, mineral and gemstone is different from the next, as different as we are to each other, and yet we are all people. We all have individualities, and when in contact with one another this must be taken into account for successful communication. Crystals are no different. With this in mind there are a few generalities to remember. Use these as a guide only; as always, you must find the best method of using crystals to suit your own needs.

Crystal healing does *not* give the user a sudden burst of unrivalled strength or foresight; it does not make anyone a superbeing. Nor does it act like kryptonite on Superman!

Usually, but not in every case, crystal healing is a gentle and subtle process, releasing energies within yourself. There are few overnight results, mainly because the effects are deep. A crystal won't suddenly cure you of all aches and pains and make you a stronger person, but it can affect you gradually, from deep within. In today's world, with convenience at our fingertips, this may be difficult to appreciate, but you must take time for the appreciation to be lasting.

It is a common misconception that crystals and minerals can do all the work for a person; this is not true. We must all put effort into their use for their full benefit to be felt. It is by our own efforts we are measured. Crystals, minerals and stones are the tools we use to gain greater understanding, but we must have the will to understand and the ability to use what we know. The effort is all ours, and we must have an open mind to allow them to work.

Experiment until you are satisfied, but always remember:

♦ Crystals, minerals and stones must *not* be taken internally. This may seem obvious – but you'd be surprised at misconceptions.

♦ The power of such materials will be of most benefit in the hands of a skilled healer. Do experiment – the fewer restrictions the better. But experiment sensibly and with an open mind.

♦ Crystals, minerals and precious stones should not be used on their own to treat serious conditions, but may be used in conjunction with other medical practices.

♦ When dealing with something new, failure will be probable if there are too many restrictions. 'Keep your mind open' is one of the most important pieces of advice. If your mind is closed you will not be sensitive to the subtleties of the energy flows. Depending on the materials, such energy flows may be subtle indeed. Free your mind from adult misconceptions and social conditioning; free yourself from entwined restrictions and benefit from life.

♦ If the crystal or stone is strongly coloured the colours could be an integral part of the power potential, so should be in view to have an effect. Hold the crystal in the hands and concentrate on the colour; clear the mind of disturbances and be open to the potential. Likewise, you may wish to wear any crystal or mineral around your neck as a pendant – an increasingly popular method of protection. Placing a crystal in a pocket is almost as good, but it is best if you can see the crystal and it can touch your skin.

♦ The power of crystals is finite, and at some stage will be in need of regeneration. Some crystals may be partially or fully regenerated by placing them in the sun – this is good for some sorts of quartz. There may be a benefit from some of these crystals, therefore, by placing them in a window. This can have the added effect of affecting anything and anyone within the room without much conscious effort. Crystals almost always work best through the subconscious.

♦ More extensive regeneration of crystals may occur if placed close to full-coloured amethyst. The amethyst can act as a 'charger' of energy so the more amethyst around a crystal the better. An amethyst geode (a hollow) open to the sun is probably the most beneficial. You will know by touch when the crystal has fully regenerated.

♦ Natural water contains many minerals, and with the addition of bath salts a person can relax and soak away tensions, anxieties and weariness. To take this a stage further it might be of benefit to place some crystals and minerals in water, for instance the calcites. Hopefully the crystals and minerals will then transfer their energies to the water in which you could bathe or simply wash. This is really no different to adding bath salts, but with those there is no specificity to you as an individual.

♦ The tools of crystal healing may at first seem a bewildering variety of shapes and colours. Becoming used to this is a matter of preference and practice. Have patience, and knowledge will be yours. One of the initial choices when confronted by the array of crystals and minerals, and especially precious stones, is whether to choose the rough, uncut samples or the cut and polished ones. The latter would seem to have the most attraction; they are pretty and pleasing to the eye and glisten to attract the magpie in us all. Certainly for jewellery purposes they are more valuable this way, and some crystals are naturally perfectly shaped and polished.

Many people, however, prefer the uncut varieties, because this is the natural state of the materials, the state in which most of the powers are retained. These powers cannot be refined and polished in the way the gems are polished; only the *use* of the powers may be refined. Touch the uncut varieties and feel their virgin life. The cut and uncut samples each have their place, but do not dismiss the rougher stones out of hand.

♦ Don't give up! Some minerals may take some time to work to your satisfaction, others act subtly or subconsciously, or you may simply have a lot of stress to relieve. Be patient; impatience will get in the way. The object of crystal healing is to relax you as a person, to allow the true you to emerge. This can only be done by a willing participant whose mind is open and clear. There is much to discover and, believe me, it will be worth the effort.

13

CHAPTER THREE

Some Useful Crystals

*T*HERE are many minerals throughout the world, only some of which have retained their energies to a useful degree. Contained in these pages are a number of the best-known healing crystals and minerals. They are by no means the only ones and must be seen only as a point from which to start your quest for greater knowledge and understanding. Only those willing to seek will find.

Human curiosity knows no bounds, yet it is frequently severely restricted. This usually begins in childhood, with fears progressively hidden deep in the mind throughout our adult years. At times, although these fears may be well hidden from scrutiny, they are hardly hidden from thought, and tend to influence people in varying degrees, in a severe instance crippling a personality. We all wish to be free. We all know we have more to give the world. We all know we have more life in us then we are permitted to display. Permitted? By what or whom? We permit ourselves by social conditioning, we restrict ourselves too much, and deep down we pay the price, as stress builds from too many chains. The freedom we seek is a freedom from our own restrictions. We must recognise this.

Crystal healing acts with subtlety and so is good at edging towards the dark areas of the mind and spirit to the source of a problem, releasing stress and tension, opening the mind and heart and freeing the spirit. Only when this is accomplished may great things be achieved, but above all, you must want to achieve them. Only you can have the will for you to succeed. Life is an incredible array of experience and wonder – it is well worth living before we die. Do not waste time, because time is what our lives are made of. Experiment – do not confine yourself!

Agate THE SAGITTARIAN

A fine-grained variety of quartz (*see page 77*), fashioned from bubbles of silica (quartz) minerals from gases and solutions rich in minerals, caught in magma (hot molten rock). As the bubbles cooled deep underground, crystals from the solutions grew inwards. The larger the crystals, the slower the cooling rate and the greater the amount of minerals within the bubbles. Agate is said to hold many of the qualities of a true fire stone – compare obsidian (*see page 67*). Within deep fires true hearts are forged – the strength of agate has carried good fortune and courage with it through the ages.

Agate is often seen with a number of different layered colours, creating a striking natural display. Agate is a true fire stone and is said to build a fire deep within a person, uncovering courage and fortitude one may not even realise is there. Such a stone can only uncover what is already there – it cannot create, but allows the deep person to shine through the doubts and confusion, to feel conviction and know what they feel is not wrong. There is a sense of pride in this. Agate allows a person to discover what there is to be discovered, to accept things with a brave heart, to strengthen the mind and body for greater trials, to calm the person in preparation. Agate is a stone for every age of mankind, its history entwined with good fortune. Courage and good fortune are always required. Some things never change.

This is why agate is called the Sagittarian (or the Fire Stone). Sagittarians are said to be strong and courageous, loyal and honest, adventurous and courteous – as well as restless and at times very, very indiscreet. Sagittarius is also a star sign. There seems to be some connection here. However, like all star signs, Sagittarius has links with a number of stones, such as turquoise (*see page 95*), malachite (*see page 62*) and amethyst (*see page 22*). At the end of this book I list some well-known birthstones. These can vary depending on the time of birth. As there can be a wide variation in birthstones, do not worry if some of them seem unfamiliar.

Throughout our lives we all undergo trials – some large, some small, some as huge as mountains and as deep as the ocean. But the huge mountains of ages past have been eroded by time; the oceans have come and gone. The physical world changes as does our own personal world, and it would be a mistake to think we live in isolation from each other or the environment. The personal trials of life are subject to the same disintegration as the mountains; it may take a long time but doubtless it will happen. With courage no individual's problems are insurmountable and good fortune is in demand.

The deep earthiness and fire of agate may be physically employed by some people to assist deep physical conditions within their own bodies, at times specifically relating to the colon and circulatory system. Agate is looked upon as being beneficial to the whole of the deep body – the whole must always be treated. At all times there must be a holistic view, which links with the deep welling of energy released by agate.

Agate sparkles with life – and life is precious. (*See photograph page 53.*)

$\mathcal{A}$*lexandrite*   THE MEANDERING GEM

This transparent relation of the gemstone beryl (*see page 27*) has a greenish colour by natural daylight but a deep red by artificial light. This difference may give rise to a different shade of potential, depending on the place of use.

Severe trauma often affects not only the mind but also the body and the spirit and can have disastrous effects. In a gentle, unimposing way, alexandrite has been known to have a beneficially passive effect on the nervous system. This may prove essential if all that is required is time to think, to reflect. In the same manner alexandrite may be recommended to help rebuild the structures of the inner self following a specific bout of turmoil or emotional exhaustion. This helps to synchronise the emotional and other psychological aspects of life for greater joy, to ensure a greater appreciation of life inside and outside oneself. Let the turbulence be banished.

All too often people think they can carry on as pressure continues to rise. Not only is this unnecessary, but it is unhelpful. We are people not machines. We all need some help along the way. Alexandrite is

MBER

TEKTITE

UBY

AMAZONITE

PPHIRE

MALACHITE

GALITE

TOURMALINE

ULEXITE

PUMICE

ALEXANDRITE

QUARTZ

BERYL

SELENITE

MOTHER OF PEARL

SERPENTINE

called the 'meandering gem' because like a slow river it makes its way in an unhurried fashion through the fabric of your inner space and time, calming, caressing troubled thoughts, soothing and healing. You need not even know it is there but like a lingering melody it will pervade every part of you and so, when you least expect it, you will be smiling through the rain and you will know there are good times ahead. The passivity of alexandrite is a subtlety verging on the sublime and maintains the sensitivity such a personality requires. (*See photograph page 18.*)

Amazonite THE ATTENTIVE ONE

This blue-green or green microcline feldspar mineral, sometimes known as amazonstone, can help soothe the nervous system. This occurs almost on a different level to alexandrite and lives up to its name as the 'attentive one' as it can comfort you and release restrictions from around yourself, to bring a sense of awareness and especially of creativity.

In today's world, with its rush and crush, the 'attentive one' could prove an essential component of survival for those who feel everyday life has subdued them or robbed them of vital imagination. Without imagination a person is stagnant and will wither from the inside out. With imagination there really are no limits, no boundaries – you may achieve your dreams and beyond. The world is full of dos and don'ts, with fears and worries, stresses and strains, yet all that exists are misunderstandings to understand and unknowns to know – all there ever is, is life. There is never anything to be afraid of, but there is a very great need to be alive, and if there is too much of a 'crush' it may seem as if life is a constant struggle.

Take time. Amazonite has been said to be able to set people on the path of true personal greatness simply by returning to them their limitless imagination. However, amazonite can also give a sense of loyalty to one's friends. Friends are always important. This mineral is attentive to detail, personal detail. It will allow you to see yourself as you truly are, to place into a correct perspective the stresses and strains of your life before they completely swamp you. Creativity is often a sign of an active life. It is often the first casualty when stress is imposed. It cannot reach the surface, yet continues within oneself, ensuring a chaos manifesting itself either in a numbing apathy or a short-fused frustration. As amazonite reduces the chaos to manageable energies, creativity returns – this is always the first sign that internal health is returning.

Creativity, imagination, foresight are essential building blocks of humanity and human nature. If any are imprisoned or lost amid the chaos of modern day life, the person runs the risk of becoming less than they were. With your help amazonite can return the pure light of life so essential and sensitive to true human nature. It is always important to be sure of who we are.

Other feldspars are moonstone (*see page 66*), and labradorite, which may have an iridescent play of colours in which blue and green predominate. (*See photograph page 17.*)

Amber   THE ANACHRONISM

Amber is the resin from fossil trees that has attained a greater stability because of relatively rapid burial underground and the volatilisation (vaporising abilities) of some constituents. In this wider sense amber represents a crossover, a link between the harnessed power of the sun and the heavy pressures of the depths of the Earth.

Amber can be found in many places throughout the world. It occurs most extensively around the edges of the shallow Baltic Sea in buried deposits between two and 65 million years old.

On occasion, opaque white amber may be found, but usually the colour ranges from yellow to brown. As the original resin exuded from a tree, the sticky material – as it then was – may have engulfed small insects or pieces of plant which then became fossilised as the resin was transformed into amber.

Because of this transformation amber is said to have a certain timelessness about it. It is said to be helpful for those wishing to recall past times, even past lives, and on occasion to help absent-mindedness. They are all linked. Amber works through the subconscious, where time has less meaning than for the conscious mind. In this way it may be seen to work with the fourth dimension of time or as a releaser of memories, a key to unlock the door. What mysteries are there to be discovered? Time and memory are, of course, great mysteries. Time is one of the building blocks of the universe. Even physicists would agree that time is not a linear phenomenon but is capable of bending as it weaves through the fabric of space, maybe to loop back on itself, to touch what has been or what will be.

In some way amber may itself touch upon this mystery on a very personal level. Where this can lead is very dependent on the individual, but have you ever dreamt of past lives? Have you ever felt you'd been somewhere before, yet knew you couldn't have been? – not in this life anyway.

Reincarnation is a fascinating subject and too large for these pages. Many people have their tales to tell, yet many others remain unconvinced, and as always it is up to the individual to believe what they want to believe. Yet we come into the world and we know not who we are; tricks of memory are nearly always put down to flights of fancy. In some areas of life and beyond there is so little understanding, but some people have a great willingness to learn and to understand, while others are afraid of what they might find. Fear can be very self-destructive.

Time is such a fascinating mystery – one which may for ever remain so, who can say? What are required are open minds and much exploration outside and inside ourselves. There is no problem that is impossible to overcome. Indeed, as time, that inescapable and inexplicable phenomenon, bends and weaves and rolls ceaselessly on, it may be possible to touch its depths. We have only to find out how, but will not find out if we are afraid. Nothing is impossible. Over the last 50 years we must at least have glimpsed this.

As in many aspects of crystal healing, the full potential of amber is largely unexplored. What is known, however, is that amber can fire the curiosity and lead you where you've never been before. Surely this is a challenge worth accepting? It is fortunate then that some sources also state that amber is good for the heart, because what shocks there would be if a mystery as vast as time was suddenly laid bare to us. And yet human curiosity knows no bounds.

The oddities of time have plagued us through the centuries. The energies of people past can hold on to stonework, on to very specific places, through time. This isn't a lingering but an active participation. Surely, therefore, we can have an effect on time? Time doesn't know we exist – it isn't an entity – yet if ghosts can persist through time perhaps this is where time touches upon itself, touching the past and the future together. Recognising that such places, such instances do not last for ever in our ever-fluid universe, perhaps we can use them for answers of our own. With amber and selenite (*see page 85*) there may be a chance it can be done.

Mathematically, physicists have shown there to be more than the four dimensions we are used to (including time). We do not know what lies beyond the unseen barriers, and are at the mercy of fertile imaginations, yet time is likely to play a part in them all. Understanding time will open many doors and life will never be the same again. Where there is a will there is a way.

True, it is our physical selves which are more concerned with time – our spiritual selves may well be endless, who can say? Certainly our spiritual selves know more of what lies beyond the borders of light and dark, and yet as we come into the world we do not know who we are; renewed, we forget. Amber can unlock the forgetfulness. It is a temptation too great to resist. (*See photograph page 17.*)

Amethyst   THE ELEVATOR

A variety of quartz (*see page 77*) this transparent purple semi-precious gem is known to many people in its natural state from its colour and arrangements of quartz crystals. Amethyst is a favourite for many types of crystal healing, because of the wide powers it is said to possess, alongside the quartz-like relegation of negativity. Amethyst is looked upon as one of the principle energisers of the mind, body and spirit, and is seen as a very powerful overall aid, able to transcend those areas. This is typical of a quartz-type reaction following the dispelling of negative energies. Amethyst, however, takes a step beyond this.

Amethyst is a very physical gem. It can have a beneficial effect on the right-hand side of the brain, which in turn translates to other, more creative energies. It is also utilised as a cleanser of the blood and an enhancer of glandular activities, especially those associated with the brain.

Spiritually it may be used for meditation purposes, as it can allow the deep part of oneself to well up, to be elevated through the superficial skin we all dwell beneath. In the right hands amethyst may free inspiration to a very great degree, like waves welling from the deep to race across the surface of an ocean and crash against those fragile cliffs of civilised learning. Amethyst can elevate above the mundane to give you an unsurpassed sense of freedom. This is what it is best known for. Amethyst energy is sharp, the colour deep and hidden, full of shadows and shades and barely understood power. It holds the pull of the unknown – a fascination.

Widely used, yet like amber not fully explored, it is essential to find a good piece of amethyst. For general protection, where the crystals are in a pocket, this is not so important, but for in-depth healing and perhaps exploration it is important to 'have the tools for the job'. The size may vary, but the larger the piece the more energy is focused. However, the crystals should be well defined and full of colour.

Increasingly, amethyst is being used for regenerative purposes; when other crystals become depleted of energy after much use, they will feel drained. When placed next to or on amethyst, and especially in the presence of pure unshielded sunlight, the amethyst is capable of focusing energy into the other crystal, regenerating it for further use.

As crystal healing is growing in recognition and popularity, the natural supply of amethyst has become stretched. To expand this natural output, it is a favourite trick of some of the more unscrupulous suppliers (who supply to some wholesalers) to heat-treat quartz to temporarily transform it into amethyst or citrine (*see page 38*). This is only a temporary transformation lasting up to several months and is largely undetectable, except that the energy levels of the amethyst may not feel quite right because of the internal confusion caused by the trickery. To the unwary the only outward sign that something isn't quite right is when the amethyst colour begins to fade following a month or two of use. Certainly if you try to regenerate other crystals using this temporary amethyst, you are likely to have to wait a long time. (*See photograph page 54.*)

Apache tears THE DEFENDER

Apache tears are globules of translucent black obsidian (*see page 67*).

They are found in Arizona and other parts of the United States, and are composed of the minerals feldspar, hornblende, biotite and quartz.

A form of volcanic glass, they were formed by rhythmic crystallisation which produced a separation of light and dark materials into spherical shapes.

The name comes from a legend about a massacre of Pinal Apache warriors in Arizona. The sadness of the women who mourned them was said to be so great that the Great Father embedded their tears into black obsidian stones, which when held to the light, reveal the translucent tear of the Apache. It is said that whoever owns an Apache tear need never cry again, for the Apache women have shed their tears in place of theirs.

Apache tears are said to have powers of protection and luck, as well as those ascribed to obsidian itself. They are therefore carried as amulets and good luck charms.

An Apache tear has energising powers; use it for healing, exorcism, intellectual powers, success, willpower and self-confidence. It is said to produce clear vision and increase psychic powers.

With Saturn its planetary ruler, it is useful for grounding and centring a personality, and for purification.

Of the elements it is related to fire, so utilise it for physical strength, energy and courage. Black obsidian is a powerful stone for meditation, bringing to light what is hidden from the conscious mind. It dissolves and purifies suppressed negative patterns, and is said to be able to create radical changes in behaviour, as positive attitudes replace former negative, egocentric ones. (*See photograph page 36.*)

Aquamarine THE QUIET ONE

This is a pale blue gemstone of the beryl family (*see page 27*) found in pegmatite, a coarse-grained igneous rock – rock formed by magma or lava that has solidified; 'igneous' comes from the Latin *igneus*, meaning fire. Due to the relatively slow cooling of the pegmatite from its molten state, it is not uncommon to find very large crystals of aquamarine.

Aquamarine is called 'the quiet one' because of its use in inspiring serenity, peace and love, states of sublime understanding we all require lest we be engulfed by chaos and lose ourselves. As a result of this greater understanding, less fear is likely to be experienced and more personal creativity. In this sense aquamarine may be of use to artists and those wishing to express themselves in a full and unique manner.

Physically aquamarine may be seen as a calmer of nervous conditions caused by the chaos of fear, that darkness we must all confront if we are to appreciate the warmth of light. Aquamarine can also be a strengthener of the major internal organs by its expulsion of chaos – a cleansing action and mirror image to its psychological effects.

In spite of its name – derived from the gem's colour only – aquamarine is a deep Earth crystal and so has the ability to affect deep problems. Chaos – that barbarian part of us we seek to exclude in order to reach a higher plane of existence – runs deep in us all. Yet as we have so much to blame the barbarian part of ourselves for, we also have much to thank it for, and it is such a part of us, our history, our very being, our very human striving for the future, what will become of us if it is tamed completely?

As there is light so there is darkness; as there is order so there is chaos. Each has its place, and without one there will be no appreciation of the other. Would we love life so much if we could never die? What is required is a balance, an understanding. Outright condemnation may well be as barbarian a trait as the barbarian act itself. Aquamarine may help maintain the balance and so aid understanding – a useful tool in any age of humanity.

Of use to artists and those wishing to express themselves, aquamarine requires a sense of humanity. Expression and humanity often go hand in hand, and with the growth of one, like a crystal growing slowly and gathering energy, there will be an appreciation of the other. This ability is within each of us, but from time to time may require some gentle nurturing to gain full benefit. Aquamarine may do this. (*See photograph page 72.*)

Aventurine   THE SEARCHER

This is a translucent gem variety of either quartz (*see page 77*) or plagioclase feldspar. Feldspar, alkali or plagioclase, is the most important rock-forming group of minerals, and accounts for approximately 60 per cent of the Earth's crust. Feldspar is a vital constituent of igneous rock. Aventurine has a spangled appearance due to small amounts of haematite (*see page 48*) and/or mica, flakes of a silicon-rich mineral able to split perfectly to form small flat sheets or plates (*see page 64*).

The quartz/haematite combination is potentially a very powerful and energetic one, but because of its composition the energy levels of aventurine tend to be most concerned with the spiritual level, which is far less limited than the physical level. Aventurine may allow a person to find their psychological and spiritual 'feet'. This can be achieved by stripping away anxiety to allow the person to see exactly where and who they are. This in turn may allow a sense of independence, translating itself into better health stemming from a more positive outlook. This has been the goal of many people for a very long time and should not be underestimated. A freeing of personal restrictions, especially if deep negativity is involved, will lift an incredible weight from a person's shoulders.

Physically aventurine may stimulate muscle tissue that has not been in use for some time, giving a sense of liveliness. However, this well-being may be as a direct result of this gem's main power on the brain and thought processes.

Aventurine may be used by those who feel confused and muddled, who wish to find their own direction through the whirlwind of life. Thus aventurine may also dispel frustration and aggression and, as the weight is lifted, the person will see the true worth of life and recognise there is nothing more glorious. (*See photograph page 35.*)

Azurite   THE DECISIVE ONE

This is a deep blue mineral whose primary metal constituent is copper. Azurite is found in the upper areas of copper ore deposits where oxygen has had a chemical effect. Usually found in conjunction with malachite (*see page 62*), the most compact areas of azurite give rise to the semi-precious stones we more commonly associate with it.

Copper is known to increase the efficiency of energy levels through-out the mind and body. It is an energetic metal unused to the gentle subtleties of some minerals and crystals. It may well be the copper content of this gem which increases the pattern of energy throughout the body, so strengthening the flow of blood and the greater dispersal of oxygen and nutrients. In this way azurite may be beneficial to those who have been without exercise for some time.

However, it is said to have a more potent power. Much like its effect on the muscles, azurite may have a greater effect on the 'psychological muscles', especially those that have lain unused. This can result in an 'awakening', which may prove startling or may be a gradual process, depending on any internal confusion and stress. The end result is the same, regardless of the length of time required. Good things are worth waiting for.

The end result may be manifested by a greater psychological ability – strong and decisive decision-making as you flex your 'psychological muscles', enhancing your control on your world. Do not surrender your responsibilities by default. Azurite may therefore be of benefit to those who find decisions difficult or have to make difficult decisions. It is likely to be of benefit to those who have been under a cloud of apathy for too long and have felt life pass them by. The energy of azurite inspires life, a love and appreciation of life. Some people are shocked by this energy, some drink it in like water in a desert, some feel no effects whatsoever. We are all different.

As in all things, the ability is always within. Gems such as azurite simply serve as a focus, clearing away disturbances to show your true ability, to be recognised and utilised to its full undepleted potential. You must always be patient and have an open mind. (*See photo page 72.*)

Beryl THE ENERGISER

Beryl is a semi-precious form of quartz (*see page 77*) with a hexagonal crystalline form, found in granite or granite pegmatites. Its green variety is emerald (*see page 43*), and it can also be yellow, blue or red. It has a glassy lustre and varies from translucent to transparent.

Like all stones of receptive energies, beryl is soothing and de-stressing. It is said to have powers of healing, love and energy, and has long been used to increase psychic awareness; it was called 'the stone of the seer'.

Lovers should exchange beryl stones to strengthen their relationship, or you should wear it to attract love.

Wear it, too, to avoid psychic manipulation or persuasion; in this sense it is said to make its bearer unconquerable, to assuage fear, and increase optimism and happiness. It is also said to help you gain understanding and retain information.

Utilise it to stop gossip, and if you are feeling lazy, hold or wear beryl and let its energy enter your body.

Beryl's planetary ruler is the moon and its elemental ruler water, and ancient people used it in rituals to bring rain. It is also said to bring protection from storms, drowning and even sea-sickness.

In healing it is considered excellent for the relief of liver complaints, swollen glands and eye diseases. (*See photograph page 18.*)

Bloodstone   THE GIVER

This variety of chalcedony silica (*see page 34*) has a cryptocrystalline structure, that is, the crystals are so finely divided that individual crystals cannot be distinguished even under a microscope. In the case of bloodstone the cryptocrystalline structure gives rise to a compact and at times waxy appearance.

Agate (*see page 15*) is also composed of bands of chalcedony, giving it its distinctive appearance. Those people sensitive to subtle energies can at times feel the original creative energies of this mineral, which seems to be the most pronounced of all the chalcedony family.

It is logical to assume that some of the powers of agate are shared by bloodstone. While this may seem the general case, the potential abilities of agate are, of course, greater than bloodstone, the latter at times being quite specific.

Whereas agate may assist courage over a wide spectrum, bloodstone is seen more as assisting the foundations of such courage – relieving stress, increasing inspiration, allowing the flow of creativity – in short, opening the eyes to give way to the wider courage of agate. However, the greater specificity of bloodstone should not be underestimated or lightly dismissed in favour of agate. Where agate has a wide spectrum of power, the energy of bloodstone is more concentrated and specific, and this may be what is required.

The main effects of bloodstone may well be the physical ones as the body prepares itself for an increase in active courage to meet the trials of life. Such preparation may begin with a strengthening of the blood vessels, progressing to the blood itself to ensure a more efficient oxygen-carrying capacity. In this way bloodstone is similar to haematite (*see page 48*), yet it can go beyond this into the heart and especially the bone marrow, which produces red blood cells (at a rate of 1.5 million per second).

The body is full of intricacies, some of which work at an incredible rate. It is only logical that some specific energy levels decline, and this can open the way to all sorts of problems. The specificity of bloodstone may prevent an energy decrease. The end result of utilising its powers could prove to be enhanced vitality, physically and mentally. (*See photograph page 54.*)

Bornite THE PEACOCK STONE

As a minor ore of copper, bornite is not a rare stone, but crystals of it are, and are considered to hold significant powers. If one were to split a piece of peacock ore, the freshly exposed surfaces would show a definite bronze colour. In the presence of oxygen this colour quickly alters to a purple iridescence, from which the name peacock comes.

As bornite is a copper ore, not surprisingly there will be an effect on the energy levels within the body. Whereas azurite (*see page 26*) may be seen as having a psychological effect and malachite (*see page 62*) as being more physical, bornite touches on the spiritual. Somehow seen as the 'ugly-duckling' of these copper minerals, bornite can lead to some surprises.

Being almost the opposite of lepidolite (*see page 60*) in its effects, the spiritual energy brought forth from chaos by the peacock stone is most often manifested in an increase of all things, including curiosity. The intellect has then been stimulated. In a purely intellectual pursuit, the energies released are likely to cause a period of spiritual instability until a new equilibrium has been attained. The cause of this temporary instability is the questioning of oneself and the things one believes.

This is a track leading to a higher awareness, and the ability to answer many of the fundamental questions of life. This is important for those seeking to find themselves, seeking a way out of the chaos. At some point in our lives we all need to do this. Few are immune from the chaos, fewer still are immune from self-doubt and questioning. On occasions, however, such a track may lead one to a greater wilderness. Bornite can help prevent this. From a spark of curiosity a great knowledge, if nurtured, can grow, as the long inner journey continues. The person on this quest to find themselves must have or achieve the ability to utilise the knowledge, however, or the journey will have been wasted.

Less dramatic than azurite or malachite, this underestimated mineral may in fact have a more profound effect on your life, as it opens up the spiritual part of yourself to question. Do you dare accept the challenge of finding out who you really are? Only when we discover who we are may we find out what we will be – and the future holds an irresistible attraction for us all. (*See photograph page 36.*)

Calcite   THE LEVELLER

This is mainly composed of calcium carbonate and is the main constituent of chalk, limestone and marble. Calcite is widely distributed throughout the world. Production continues as a natural process, mainly of aquatic life.

The mineral is initially produced by a number of aquatic invertebrates as an essential component of their shells. When the invertebrates die the shells sink, and *en masse*, over time, collect on the sea bed. As long as the shells do not progress to the dark abyssal depths of the oceans they will remain relatively undissolved. Over a period of time, as they gather, they may be buried and turned into the forms of calcite we are able to recognise. This means that calcite is a true gatherer of the energies of the oceans and the seas, of the waves and the life therein – the mysterious depths beneath an unsure surface.

Calcite continues to be created. The forms of rock from this mineral that we see today were set down in ancient seas, most of it long before man walked upon the earth.

The white cliffs of Dover are perfect examples of billions and billions of calcium carbonate shells from millions of years ago, now seen as chalk. Limestone tends to be harder than this soft chalk, showing the more rigorous processes it has undergone. Sometimes limestone may be interspaced by thin bands of mudstone, indicating when the even floor of invertebrate shells was disturbed by usually more rapid accumulations of mud. The world is, and always has been, in a state of flux. We live so few years we fail to notice most of what happens by slow processes.

With the to and fro of tides powered by the gravitational attractions of the moon and sun, with great density-driven currents moving water through every ocean, with constant volcanic activity along huge oceanic ridges pushing the continents apart and together, the ocean is a harvester of immense energies. The ocean is also a good balancer of energies, and calcite follows this. Calcite cannot exist at the great depths of an ocean, and so its main energy potential does not work at great depths within a person. This may be what is required. For example, if there is an unhappiness it may be due to present circumstances; there may not be a deep cause.

Calcite can have the ability to reduce the irrationalities of stress and fear, as well as those of the other extreme of over-enthusiasm. Like the sea, calcite can inspire a calm happiness, a peacefulness, a freedom from heaviness, a lightness few may be able to experience. In essence it can balance the extremes to find a very acceptable and very personal midpoint for your satisfaction. This can resolve any internal conflict and lead to a harmonious equilibrium before any chaos reaches the depths to settle in a great confusion.

Physically, the energies of calcite may manifest themselves in a benefit to the kidneys or the other internal organs which are affected by emotional extremes. For make no mistake, stress is a killer in every sense of the word.

The composition and healing power of calcite is very close to coral (*see page 40*), so please use calcite rather than the severely endangered coral. (*See photograph page 71.*)

Carnelian   THE AMIABLE ONE

Sometimes known as cornelian, this is a translucent semi-precious type of chalcedony (*see page 34*), with close links to the variety known as sard (*see page 84*). Carnelian has a reddish colour as a result of colloidal (suspended) haematite (*see page 48*) dispersed throughout.

With its close connections to agate (*see page 15*), carnelian also may enhance physical and psychological well-being, allowing energies to find their way to the surface more readily without the turmoil and chaos of being locked within. Carnelian is seen as an organiser of emotions – another foundation for the courage agate can enhance, for without organisation there is only chaos, and it is chaos we seek to elevate ourselves from. Only by this means may we truly find the peacefulness of knowledge and certainty. Only by this means may a heart be sure.

Such organisation can result in a greater ability to concentrate, for whatever end you see fit. Concentration demands energy. The haematite content of carnelian can free locked energy, whereas the chalcedony channels it. This is potentially a very powerful combination of benefit to a wide variety of people, because we all undergo bouts of chaos and confusion, some more than others. During times of severe stress a lack of concentration often makes matters worse.

Physically, carnelian may enliven the internal organs and hasten the regeneration of tissues. This can be seen as a purely physical result of an emotional balance. But more than this, because of the presence of haematite, carnelian may energise the blood, specifically the oxygen-carrying red blood cells, which will bring benefit to most parts of the body.

In dealing with the confusion of everyday life carnelian is a largely overlooked gem, and it is this confusion it seeks to alleviate. (*See photograph page 71.*)

Cat's eye THE BEAUTIFIER

This is the name given to several stones, usually a quartz (*see page 77*) containing olive-green asbestos. The term 'cat's eye' refers to the green 'eye' effect that emerges when a stone is polished. The term can also be applied to several types of polished obsidian, and to beryl.

Variants of cat's eye are tiger's eye (*see page 92*), which is golden brown, and hawk's eye, which is blue. However, the ancient Asian cat's eye was a form of chrysoberyl.

An energising stone, cat's eye has a moving and luminous opalescence. The Assyrians believed it caused invisibility, probably because of its dazzling appearance.

32

It is said to be powerful in matters to do with wealth and gambling, but also in protection and healing. Its planetary ruler is Venus, and so it is also used as a beauty aid; wear or carry it to increase beauty and preserve youthfulness.

It is said to be useful in matters of mental health, insight and luck, and is said to dispel depression and give pleasure.

Because of its eye-like appearance, it is considered to help diseases of the eyes.

Celestite   THE STONE OF HEAVEN

Although the term 'stone of heaven' has much to do with celestite's name, it is not merely a superficial confusion. Celestite in its natural form did not fall from the heavens and it was not handed down by any gods. It is an orthorhombic mineral born from the processes that continue to shape the Earth. (Orthorhombic is a type of crystal system. The other basic systems are cubic, tetragonal, hexagonal, monoclinic and triclinic.) Celestite contains significant amounts of strontium. Perhaps because of this celestite may prove to be of benefit to the bones. However, it must be stated that any benefit here may only be slight, as the main potential of this mineral tends to work through the less physical paths.

Psychologically and spiritually, celestite may calm the chaos of internal turbulence, giving peace of mind. This in turn could allow a measure of spiritual growth as you become aware of a higher plane of existence and, with human curiosity, reach through the dimensions, gathering truth like snowflakes, knowledge like dust. Through the turbulence it will show you a light. It is the light of your own life – see how brightly it shines.

Celestite can give clarity. This is what it is best known for. Throughout the centuries people have striven to reach a higher existence. This requires more than courage, more than organisation of the emotions; it requires foresight and the readiness to accept. Celestite can give clarity to see not only ourselves but the world as we do not know it. In this way it must be a worthwhile ally if we are to reach beyond our grasp to that which we know is there. Minerals such as agate and celestite often work well together to enable us to reach beyond ourselves, almost beyond our human existence, earthbound and restricted.

Celestite may not be from the heavens, but it can surely help us to reach there – if that is what we wish to reach. Creatures of such celebrated imperfection as we often dream of perfection as an answer to all our problems. Yet, think of this, if we were all perfect, time would weigh heavily upon us and there would be little enough mystery left. Be careful what you wish for, as it may come true. (*See photo page 71.*)

Chalcedony   THE PACIFIER

A translucent quartz gemstone (*see page 77*), conchoidal (shell-like) and of hexagonal crystalline form, it can be grey, blue-grey or yellow-grey, with a vitreous silky lustre.

Chalcedony has soothing receptive energies, and is ruled by the moon and the element water. Use it for its powers in the areas of peace, travel, protection and luck, and against nightmares.

It is said to banish fear, hysteria, depression, sadness and mental illness. When worn or held in the hand it is thought to promote calm and peaceful feelings, prevent accidents and offer protection while travelling. If worn to bed or placed under the pillow, it is thought to drive away nightmares, night visions and fear of the dark.

It is also used for beauty, strength, energy and success, and in Italy mothers wear beads of white chalcedony to increase lactation. (*See photograph page 54.*)

Chrysocolla   THE FEMININE STONE

Associated with azurite (*see page 26*) and malachite (*see page 62*), this copper mineral is usually located in areas of copper and sulphide deposits where oxygen has had a chemical effect, usually the upper reaches of ore deposits.

Chrysocolla is known as the 'feminine stone' because of its effects on the feminine qualities. Strength is anything you wish to make it, but chrysocolla is not a weak stone. Femininity is a strength, a valuable attribute in an impersonal world, and should be seen as such, and this mineral may be used to enhance femininity while building an inner

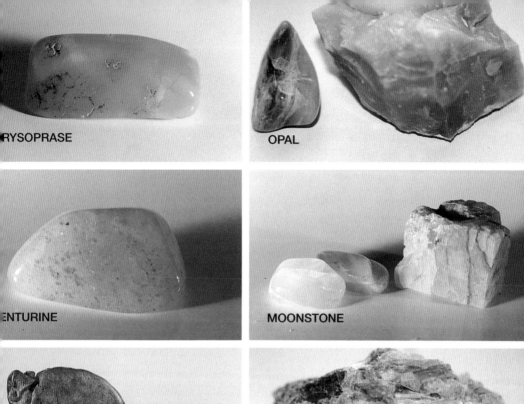

RYSOPRASE

OPAL

ENTURINE

MOONSTONE

PPER

KYANITE

ODONITE

DIOPTASE

ODOCHROSITE

DIAMOND

APACHE TEARS

MICA

BORNITE

RUTILATED QUARTZ

EMERALD

SARDONYX

GARNET

SILVER

LAVA

ZIRCON

strength and excluding fear from lack of self-confidence. Lack of self-confidence stems from our childhood and the way we see ourselves. By enhancing femininity, chrysocolla can allow a woman to feel her best and so dispel any doubts and negative thoughts about herself. This is a very important stone because all too often we are tempted to strip ourselves away for the sake of 'fitting in' with the world, whereas we should be pushing harder to make the world mould that little bit more to ourselves. Chrysocolla is also seen as helpful with pre-menstrual tension (PMT), relieving stress and tension, by helping to correct energy imbalances within the body. This may also be of use with any hormonal imbalance. The physical and psychological effects are, of course, linked.

Collectively this can result in a freer personality, allowing the inner self to shine through with a personal confidence from the knowledge that you are a woman, and without women there would be no humanity. Without men there can also be no humanity. Waging war on half the population does not lead to fairness in the long run – but neither does losing oneself. We are all important. Our differences have made the world a wonderful place, and such diversity should be protected.

Chrysocolla has an importance that is likely to grow. (*See photo page 71.*)

Chrysoprase FOR CONTENTEDNESS

This gem variety of chalcedony *(see page 34)* has a pale turquoise or bright green appearance and like all other varieties is cryptocrystalline. Because of its gem status chrysoprase can verge on the expensive.

It is seen as an introverted mineral because of the way it can aid insight into oneself. This may be used to locate other well-hidden problems and psychological scars – and to heal.

Yet the mineral may go further than this. Increasingly, it is being seen as an aid to alleviate depression caused by sexual frustration. By helping the root of the problem it may indeed produce contentedness. Logic would indicate that there has always been sexual frustration, but there is a definite indication of a significant growth in this frustration, undoubtedly due to the society we have made and which we frequently condemn. In society in general there is a growing unrest. Obviously this does not have a single cause and sexual frustration acts on a very personal level, raising the degree of personal anguish and stress. This may indeed lead to stress wider in scope.

Chrysoprase is typical of crystal healing affecting changes among a wider public. It is a useful gem, restricted only by its expense. (*See photograph page 35.*)

Citrine FOR REASSURANCE

Sometimes known as the 'cuddle quartz', citrine is a yellow-brown crystalline quartz mineral, at times the colour of topaz (*see page 93*). Indeed, the qualities of the two are also alike in some respects.

This mineral is a helpful one. In this day and age it is all too easy to forget who we really are, to forget the worth we have as individuals. When this happens self-esteem and even self-respect can suffer, and from then on there is the danger of a downward spiral into oblivion. The chaos engulfs and it may be difficult to find a way out. Even if there *is* a way out, things are likely to have changed in your personal world by the time you surface.

Citrine has the ability to give warmth where there is coldness, to give light where there is darkness, to give hope where there is desolation, to recall life. Citrine will not allow you to forget yourself. It can raise you above the turmoil to show you there is life beyond the void – a helping hand, a reassurance. Sometimes all we need is a cuddle. The remainder will be up to you. If you wish to accept this helping hand you may then strive towards fully regaining yourself, in the sure knowledge that you have great worth.

This is an incredible comfort. You will know what it means if you have ever stood alone in the cold on the edge of the great abyss. The void is a desolate place unsuitable for human contact. It is wise to retain healthy links with a society of people and not dwell in isolation. It is not 'soft' of us to want the comfort of company.

Potential physical benefits seem tame when placed beside the others. But it may be helpful to know that citrine is said to have a good effect on many internal organs, especially those related to digestion. These are undoubtedly secondary effects gained from personal comfort.

Citrine holds the cold at bay, the depths of loneliness in busy streets where people pass by each other too quickly. The rush of modern life has been imposed upon us – it would not exist without our consent, or rather our default. (*See photograph page 71.*)

Copper   THE ENERGETIC ONE

Judging by the number of people wearing copper bracelets as a means of combating rheumatism, many seem to believe in its powers. Why then might they dispute the powers of other such materials? Is copper really such a brilliant exception, or have some people, true to style, not really looked closely enough?

Copper, the pure metal and its alloys, has been in extensive use for thousands of years. Its potential is *not* a modern invention.

Sun-coloured and bright, copper may be seen as a natural energiser. Its abilities cover a wide spectrum and many copper-containing minerals such as azurite, bornite and malachite (*see pages 26, 29 and 62 respectively*), display distinct copper-like effects, but with subtle differences that go to make them individuals. The emphasis, as always with copper, must be on the body's natural energy. This is what copper can help elevate, distribute and balance – the whole energy level – physical, psychological and spiritual. Matters must always be seen in their holistic context. Any spiritual effect will result in an effect on the way the mind works and the way the body works. There is never any separation of the parts, and copper can enhance the energy links between them.

We are full of energy. At times it may not seem as if this is true, but biologically we are more efficient at converting food to fuel than the top racing car. We radiate in the infra-red, our minds are busy even when we sleep, our spirits range far beyond us. We are an energetic species and we can accomplish anything if we really want to. There is little doubt we are bound for greatness.

As the general energy level can be elevated, or rather freed, the specific effects will be manifested in specific ways, depending on the individual. The effects should be in those areas of greater need, but generally a more energetic flow of blood can be felt as the increased and released energy finds its path. This can be helpful to those burdened by a weariness they can't quite shake off, a twentieth-century malaise.

Even though we are energetic beings, it is not surprising that when confronted by the confusion of today's world, our energy levels may themselves become confused and so depleted. The apathy, the lethargy, the 'can't see any point' attitude prevailing throughout society requires the natural tonic of energetic copper. A freeing of energy is merely an exercise in efficiency, yet one which is sorely needed to experience the fullness of life and to appreciate further elevating benefits of crystal healing.

As far as specifics like rheumatism are concerned, copper will *not* work for everyone in the same way, but there are often similarities in the way it does work and in the end result. It all depends on the individual and the way their energies are distributed. Copper will *not* directly dispel the pain and discomfort of any physical ailment, but it can act indirectly by balancing energy requirements. It may often feel as if the copper is acting directly, but this is only because we are unable consciously to detect the subtle variations which may be under way in other areas. Copper, as with other healers, works on the whole, not just parts of the whole. (*See photograph page 35.*)

Coral

Some people advocate the use of this sea stone for various forms of healing and protection. This point of view verges on the callous, as the point of healing is to heal and not to destroy.

In its natural environment coral sustains an incredible and wonderful variety of life, all of which is under severe threat. The threat is essentially from tourists who wish to carry a piece of the tropics home with them, although a number of outlets in this country also stock coral jewellery and trinkets to tempt the unwary and the uncaring. Every little bit taken adds to the devastation. Coral may be beautiful to look at, but outside its natural environment it has much less beauty and worth than if left alone.

For those requiring the *potential* power of coral, it is composed of calcium carbonate – calcite (*see page 30*). In many ways calcite is close to coral, so if you require any help, please use calcite. Other minerals and crystals are also mined, but none have such a fragile network of life dependent upon them as coral. (*See photograph page 53.*)

Diamond THE MASTER STONE

This name, the 'master stone', concerns the diamond's potential powers and is not used in relation to any masculine or feminine attributes. Indeed, it is also known as 'a girl's best friend', but this has been brought about largely by commercial concerns. It is not quite true to say that diamonds are extremely rare; their rarity among the greater public has also been brought about largely by commercial interests. In fact, many of the public's perceptions of diamonds are closely linked to the commercialisation of this mining product.

Diamonds are crystalline forms of carbon. The closest mineral relation to diamond is graphite – the lead in pencils – softer than diamond due to the only real difference between them, the way the carbon atoms are arranged. Diamond is the hardest natural mineral known. It is formed in volcanic diatremes ('pipes') at least 200 km below the surface. At such a depth, the temperature and pressure within this volatile environment would be close to the extreme. The famous Kimberley diamond mines of South Africa explore an extensive diatreme. Both the colourless and the coloured diamonds are treasured as gemstones and have been valued for a long time.

Whatever the origin of the initial carbon, diamonds have been transformed into a complexity of Earth and fire stones. The depth of their potential is reflected in the depth at which they can heal. Always remember that most (though not all) life on Earth is carbon based – as we ourselves are. A basic rule in chemistry is 'like dissolves like', i.e. oil dissolves oily substances, water dissolves watery substances. This may seem obvious, but in fact has far-reaching consequences. Water cannot pass through the skin because of the oils naturally produced in the skin, yet some oils can pass through. Like dissolves like.

It's the same with the diamond. Made of carbon, it therefore has the ability to reach deeper within us than many others can go. This has its advantages. The main disadvantage, however, is that good diamonds are not easy to come by, and are highly priced because of their commercial value, which is kept as high as possible.

The 'master stone', like a master key, can open many doors. It has wide variability, purpose and potential. The purpose and depth are often defined by the individual, who may not know just how deep this carbon material can go. It has the ability to go deep, very deep. Diamonds are seen as being among the best at purifying the mind, body and the spirit of toxins, frustrations and chaos, leaving all as sparklingly clear as the most flawless diamond. This is no mean feat. If one were to stare into the heart of a diamond one would almost feel one's attention flowing inward. A diamond is known to be a powerful healer which requires little regeneration, because beneath its surface it holds on to its energies well, almost beating with the beat of your own heart, flowing with the warmth of your hand.

There is a central action to diamond. From this central clarity, emanating radially in all directions, diamond has the ability to enhance every part of a life, as its wide energies flow to every undiscovered corner of a person to calm and to heal with the fire and the pressure of its own birth. Like copper, and with every other crystal, mineral and precious stone, specifics are individual. In many cases there is likely to be a general 'lifting' of conscious perceptions and perhaps a detectable surge in subconscious activity.

Beyond such flimsy generalities the individual is likely to experience strong and overwhelming specific actions. A sceptic might say this is because of the commercial value of the diamond. The world is rarely moved by sceptics, however, but by people who try, people who want – achievers who are not put off by sceptics. Diamond is called the 'master stone' because it has the ability to achieve what it may take many minerals to achieve. What do you want to achieve? Dare to dream and it may come true. An old proverb states: 'A fair maid a faint heart never won'. (*See photograph page 35.*)

Dioptase THE SEER

Dioptase is a green transparent to translucent mineral similar to atacamite and euchroite. It has a high copper and quartz content and usually occurs in association with calcite (*see page 30*), chrysocolla (*see page 34*), malachite (*see page 62*) and/or limonite in the mineral oxidation zones (usually the upper reaches of a deposit, where oxygen affects the mineral composition). Dioptase can occur in crystals, as druses (an aggregate of crystals within a cavity), or as large-scale aggregates.

The pleasant green of this mineral is a lively colour which enhances its properties. The copper content of dioptase is the part responsible for vitalising the mind and body, sweeping the cobwebs aside with a gentle wave of energy. The quartz content is the part responsible for balancing the mind and body, smoothing out the dangerous negativities lurking in all our shadows.

Together, this combination is a powerful but gentle healing tool, having a beneficial effect initially on the nervous system and the heart through the dispelling of negativity and the enhancement of the more positive aspects.

From such benefits there is a significant likelihood of extensive secondary effects. As always, when stress is relieved, to be replaced by the healthy energy of life, an enhancement of the body's own natural equilibrium can be felt. In this way the body itself achieves stability, reducing ulcers, insomnia, high blood pressure and potentially many other stress-related ailments. This could prove very advantageous.

The psychological effects can also be extensive. This usually begins with an emotional stability, which then pervades through every aspect of the personal life. As stress is dispelled there will be a clarity from which advancement is not just possible but probable. From this point whatever happens is a purely personal achievement – but the doors will have been opened.

In life there are always opportunities. Sometimes, however, they may be obscured by circumstance and/or personal confusion. The subtle combination of copper and quartz held in dioptase crystals lends the energy and balance required for a personal progression through personal abilities unclouded by chaos.

Dioptase is an uncommon mineral, yet one well worth locating. (*See photograph page 35.*)

Emerald   THE PURE LOVE STONE

This highly prized beryl gemstone (*see page 27*), owes its green colour to the presence of the metallic element chromium. At its birth the emerald crystallises into its natural hexagonal prismatic form. This usually takes place in mica-schist rocks – metamorphic rocks with a high mica content (*see page 64*), in a well-developed parallel orientation. (Metamorphic rocks are those whose original structure and composition have been considerably altered by pressure and heat.)

Love is one of the great driving forces in human nature. It has been the death of many and the life of many more. Without it poets would be an unfulfilled lot. Love stirs the heart and blood, fires the imagination and touches ordinary people with greatness. None of us could do without it, for if we tried we would become less than human. Love is at its best when it is sure. Through the ages there have been love potions and spells and tales a-plenty. Pure love is much sought after. Emerald is often seen as the embodiment of this.

Love is often tinged with all sorts of unworthy attributes, yet the pure love stone is so-called because it often inspires purity in love. This can come about by the stone's ability to disperse with the superficial turmoil that might otherwise be blocking the natural flow of energy – deep, deep energy from beyond the physical and psychological barriers. This dispersion of turmoil can allow a person to balance any conflicts within themselves and achieve much-needed emotional stability, the basis of a lasting and worthwhile feeling of love, a warmth to wash over them, true certainty amid a world of uncertainty. What a comfort this is. Emerald has incredible potential. This potential may be fully exercised only by a person who is willing and completely receptive. The effects will then be worthwhile, for without love we are empty shells of creatures who may bear the look of humanity but fail to understand its meaning.

Emerald may also be useful in balancing the dangerous negativities of love, such as jealousy. Jealousy has an important place, yet if there is an over-abundance it often proves to be a terribly destructive force. By redistributing the energies, emerald may even this out without disturbing the passion.

Physically this gem has been known to enhance the immune system as well as the physical muscle of the heart. These, however, may be the indirect effects of being in love and being able to love with the full force and depth of humanity. It is called being free, and can work wonders on the physical being. The full force of positive behaviour can carry us to the heaven of our own making. Emerald has great potential for romantics, incurable or not.

On a practical level, the Indians of some South American forests have been known to grind small emeralds into a paste to smear across their skin as a forest camouflage cream. (*See photograph page 36.*)

Fluorite   THE GATHERER

This is commercially known as fluorspar. Depending on its purity, fluorite is a clear to transparent halide mineral (one containing halogen atoms), though a number of colours are known. Perhaps the most famous variety of fluorite is Blue John, from the Blue John caves in Derbyshire, for centuries a place of wonder.

Fluorite is a fire mineral, produced in association with the sulphides of lead, zinc and sometimes silver in high-temperature hydrothermal veins. Hydrothermal activity occurs mainly in volcanic areas; super-heated water is forced through surrounding rocks, dissolving metals and minerals. As the water cools the dissolved minerals drop out of solution at specific temperatures. This gives rise to a veined structure, the bearer of much gathered energy from numerous sources.

As would therefore be expected, fluorite, 'the gatherer', has a far-reaching potential. It can be capable not of calming but extracting excess energy from you at times when concentration or a level head is required. This is beneficial for anger or drastically impulsive behaviour, and can lead a person to take time to examine matters more closely, and to be in touch with intuition and most of all with common sense. Drastic decisions often have drastic repercussions, causing needless stress. Before stress builds up, it would be beneficial all round if the initial cause were examined in a cool, calm and collected manner.

History is full of disasters caused by drastic decisions. People's lives are so closely entwined that it is fascinating to think of the chain of events leading from a decision from someone else to the effects on oneself, effects which may well change lives. When you throw a stone into a pool, see how the ripples spread. Such are the consequences of each decision you make. Trying to be careful on behalf of other people is not simply a courteous and thoughtful thing to do, but is also likely to affect the decisions of other people, and so the effects on you yourself. No man is an island – this is a comforting thought.

Fluorite can help unblock barriers within right-hand brain activity, often a cause of confusion, frustration and anger. Once free, the right-hand side of the brain is capable of exploring and understanding the complexities of life. Take time and understand. Usually this is all that is required to appreciate the true wonder of life. (*See photograph page 54.*)

Garnet   THE DREAMER

'The dreamer' is an appropriate description of this stone, because of the wide range of constituents it can hold. Every garnet seems to possess slightly different powers, although the basic crystal structure remains the same. This means each garnet must be treated on its own merits.

All garnets have a glassy appearance. They can be found in any colour with the exception of the far end of the visible spectrum. This may indicate a low level of energy; a more subtle approach which would probably take time to work may be needed but, as always, the best things are worth waiting for.

The most commonly recognised type of garnet is a deep red; a further variety showing a red to violet colour is known as carbuncle. Garnet is a common minor accessory mineral in igneous rocks (those derived from magma or lava that has solidified on or below the Earth's surface); it is therefore no surprise to know it can often be located in metamorphic rocks.

As garnet seems to have a more subtle approach than other crystals, it may also be no surprise to learn that it is known for its properties of regeneration. Regeneration of any bodily tissues requires not only time but also a gentle touch. This power of regeneration is also seen as being able to purify. A suitable combination could be with jade (*see page 52*), and its lure of longevity.

However, with its low level of approach, garnet is probably more suited to fine tuning the emotional balance and helping to stop any potential problems before they are able to grow out of hand – sexual problems are a good example. Garnet's true potential therefore lies in its preventative action rather than in any curative powers. It is a 'just-in-case' stone. Because of this, a lot of people tend to carry small garnets around with them, usually in the original matrix. (*See photograph page 36.*)

Gold   THE SUN STONE

As gold is an earth stone fashioned by a fiery background, the name 'sun stone' comes from its standing among the ancient Aztecs and Incas of Central and South America. They believed gold was a representation of the sun's body on Earth, its power and energy. This must not be mistaken for the aventurine mineral sunstone (*see page 90*).

Gold is a relatively rare soft metal. It mostly occurs in its natural, native gold form, but alloys of silver and copper have been known. Wherever discovered it has had distinct and measurable effects on the local country.

Quite apart from any commercial concerns, gold has a purely positive effect, and this is what it is best known for within the realm of crystal healing. It does not negate negative energies out of hand, but has the ability of enhancing the positive, producing both a physical and psychological effect. This ability opens many doors – the sun always shines on the positive. Opportunities present themselves more often when you are in a positive frame of mind. Like everyone else, you experience ups and downs as life vibrates around an equilibrium. Gold heightens this fragile balance.

The physical effects of a revitalised positive attitude may be wide and varied and, as in many instances, are dependent upon the greatest need. However, the prime effect, which is known to occur prior to any other 'branching out' of positive energy, can be a quite specific enhancement of the nervous system – the whole nervous system, from the central to the peripheral. On occasions a tingling sensation may be felt as the peripheral nerves are re-awoken. If you've ever held a piece of raw gold you'll know how this feels, and the feeling isn't purely due to its potential commercial value.

An awakening of those parts of the brain heavy with dust and cobwebs will surely invigorate you, will allow a wave of perception to flood the information receptors. In this way gold has a powerful potential. However, it is undoubtedly the indirect effect on personal awareness, an internal awareness that gold can have, which seems to interest many people. Anything is possible if you want it to be – this is the message gold tries to explain to us. Why be held in place by negative restrictions when you can soar with positive energies?

The unlimited possibilities gold may then produce must make for a quest of great personal interest. Where could it lead you? What is there to discover? It is thought that the ancient Druids fashioned tools from gold for these reasons, and had lifetimes of practice to know the effects. Surrounded by negativity, we forget too easily. (*See photo page 72.*)

Haematite   THE GLOWING NIGHT STONE

Something like six per cent of the Earth's crust is composed of iron – it is widely distributed. Most living things have a use for iron. It is essential to our lives.

Haematite (often spelt hematite) is the main mineral ore of iron and can occur either in huge granular formations or as flower-like 'iron roses'. These larger formations on or near the surface may be classed as red ochre. Haematite seems to be largely formed by the process of sedimentation (settling out from bodies of water), and is known to be important in the preservation of some fossils.

Haematite is an Earth stone that has retained the energy of the deep seas. It is this mysterious mixture of depths which makes some people wary of it – it is the mystery of the unknown, a primeval fear with which we must not be burdened if we are to reach beyond the barbarous. The presence of haematite is felt by many minerals, and it is an important presence, potentially one of the most important, because of its energising nature. Haematite does not often require regeneration. Only after extensive and intensive use may some regeneration be required. The link between iron and the Earth's magnetic field may be responsible for the seemingly endless supply of energy to haematite. Little investigation has been carried out on this yet. Haematite is said to be at its most powerful at times of high solar activity, on the 11-year cycle, and at times of high activity in the atmosphere, of the *aurora borealis* (northern lights).

As with many iron minerals, the main physical energising effect is known to be on the blood. Haematite may be seen as the most advanced of these minerals, and can have a direct effect on the oxygen-carrying capacity of the blood through the very specific action of the iron on the haemoglobin. A transference of energy perhaps. As in other cases, this will have the effect of energising every area touched by blood, which in effect means the whole body, and will clear the mind to a higher state of awareness.

Such a higher state of awareness will dispel stress and encourage a positive attitude, usually in the form of optimism. From optimism energy often branches out into courage and inspiration. These may be of an energetic form and others may find it difficult to keep up with you, but don't worry, this is simply the mind readjusting to a new equilibrium and soon the flow of energy will relax to a more comfortable state, filling you with confidence. Here there is an undetectable meeting point with the powers of agate (*see page 15*), because of the presence of haematite in some forms of chalcedony within the agate.

The depths of haematite may be worth braving. The adventurous are always responsible for pushing back the frontiers of knowledge and understanding. The human spirit is at its best doing just that. (*See photograph page 54.*)

Hairstone THE STIMULATING ONE

With varieties and names such as rutilated quartz, needlestone, Venus hair (*see page 82*), sagenite and ulexite (*see page 96*), this mineral has come in for a lot of attention over the ages.

Hairstone is an interesting mineral. In its self-enclosed world of clear crystalline quartz there are often a number of hair-like or needle-like (hence needlestone) inclusions of other minerals. These can be so extensive that they present a dense tangled mass within the clear quartz, reaching between the individual quartz crystals. Hairstone is often cut and polished to enable the full clarity of the quartz and depth of the inclusions to be appreciated.

The two main inclusions are actinolite and rutile. The actinolite gives a greenish appearance; rutile gives a yellow-red-brown colour, depending on the density of inclusions. Rutile inclusions are the most common, hence the name rutilated quartz, also known as Venus hair or sagenite. The latter may also contain goethite or tourmaline.

Hairstone tends to be much sought after, with good examples able to command relatively high prices. The almost dreamlike properties of this material make such expense acceptable. Like the inclusions, the potential of hairstone works by weaving its way through every thought, every action and dream, enhancing and strengthening. In this way hairstone is capable of dismantling psychological and spiritual barriers and allowing stimulation through raised awareness. This seems to occur mostly when asleep, when the mind and spirit embrace more fully, and can temporarily escape bodily confinements. Barriers are more effectively dismantled, so when the person awakes there is an increased awareness of life, of themselves, of many matters. This may take some time to fully appreciate, as the spirit is not prone to the same vagaries of time as our physical selves.

Depending on the individual, this can have many indirect but none the less very important knock-on effects. We all must explore the world, the universe, ourselves in our own ways. Hairstone may show us that we are not frightened children standing all alone in a cold darkness. There can also be a general lessening of depression, from this dispelling of negative energies. There also seems to be a beneficial effect on that part of the brain dealing with communication, where congestion and confusion reign in many people. The barriers will be cleared, yet it takes time, so handicapped are we by having so little time to express our true nature. We are all born explorers. It is only later, with the installation of others' fears, that we are restricted.

Helictite   THE FAERIE WAND

Helictite is not a pure mineral, but a varied concoction of water-borne minerals. The potential of this stone is therefore as varied. For precise effects one must look at the surrounding rocks where the helictite originated.

Whereas stalactites and stalagmites are vertical, helictite is a branchlike, usually horizontal, growth structure, highly contorted. It is produced mainly from calcite but with many other ingredients, depending on the surrounding rocks and the passage of water. The thickness of the branch depends on the water channels, but may be as thick as an arm or more fibrous than a thread.

Many of the powers contained by helictite are similar to those of calcite (*see page 30*), but may be seen as being a magnitude weaker and therefore may be of use to those who feel they do not require the full energy of calcite.

However, the main use for helictite is said to be its potential for allowing a person to be in touch with every aspect of nature – the tree spreading its branches to catch the sun, the birds' song, the wind as it sweeps across ancient land. It is claimed that helictite allows a person's physical sensory nerves to expand (compare with lepidolite – *see page 60*) as far as they dare, through every dimension, like a network of nerve endings, which they may then explore and discover. This is not to be used by the unwary.

In folklore helictite was said to be used by half-mystical creatures such as elves and faeries. If you are familiar with the origin of the tales of such creatures and how popular misconceptions have evolved through the ages, you will see there may indeed be a grain of truth in the old stories.

Helictite is not readily available, so you may have to search hard to find some, and you will find that even a small piece is very expensive.

Herkimer diamond THE LIGHT

Herkimer diamonds, unlike true diamonds, are not pure carbon but quartz (*see page 77*). They are named after a small place in New York State, and are naturally double-terminated crystals usually found within the rock dolomite of a specific geological age. ('Double-terminated' usually refers to two well-defined points, one either end of the crystal structure.) The most perfect Herkimer diamonds tend to be less than half an inch long; larger specimens are often fractured.

Herkimer diamonds may be seen as a condensed or amplified version of normal clear quartz crystals. Their rarity in comparison to quartz often leads to substantial expense.

As with many quartz crystals there can be a notable balancing of negative energies and a significant lessening of stress. However, the amplification of Herkimer diamonds allows this potential to reach far beyond less able crystals. Herkimer diamonds lay claim to numerous abilities, many on a personal level, but unless the user has experience with crystals and minerals, it is easiest to concentrate on the amplification of the quartz abilities when utilising Herkimer diamonds.

51

Perhaps as a result of this amplification, Herkimer diamonds are said to extensively aid inner vision. Increasingly, this is what they are becoming known for, as people aspire towards a greater awareness not only of the world about them but also that within them. Knowing oneself is not a simple task, but is one which can herald substantial stability, very deep peace of mind and sure actions.

It is typical of quartz to achieve this, yet Herkimer diamonds can go further. How far? Really, the only limits are those we place on ourselves. True freedom begins within. (*See photograph page 72.*)

Jade THE PATIENT STONE

This very hard gem has its healing roots in ancient Chinese history, where it was associated with life forces and good fortune.

Jade may be composed of either the waxy jadite mineral or the very tough nephrite mineral. Both forms show a wide variety of colours, almost the full spectrum, which may give a clue to jade's range of powers.

However, if anything, jade is as subtle as garnet. Its smooth energies may take some time to work, but this is only because it pervades slowly and surely – patiently. Its power flows over and through in a slow, deliberate movement, strengthening physical attributes for a reputed increase in longevity and clarity of thought. An increase in longevity has long been a goal for many people, alchemists, wizards and modern scientists alike. Like transforming lead into gold or producing the greatest love potion, eternity has been a lure to tempt the unwary, unscrupulous and desperate. Through all of this the belief in jade has remained.

Jade allows the virtue of patience to shine through. This allows a far-reaching and level-headed approach to life, a far-sighted holistic view, much of which may be said to be lacking among those who seek to control our lives. Known also as the 'virtue stone', jade has been recognised as enhancing many virtues within an individual. These can include wisdom, the courage to be honest and the modesty that comes from a patient and sure personality. The list, if not endless, is certainly more extensive, and is dependent upon the individual.

ATE

PETRIFIED WOOD

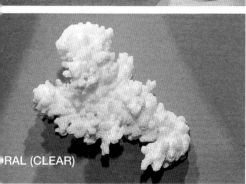

RAL (CLEAR)

ROSE QUARTZ

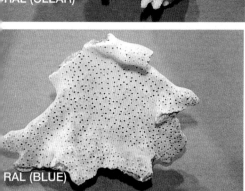

RAL (BLUE)

TOPAZ

DE

TURQUOISE

RIDOT

VARISCITE

AMETHYST

JASPER

BLOODSTONE

JET

CHALCEDONY

OBSIDIAN

FLUORITE

SMOKY QUARTZ

HAEMATITE

TIGER'S EYE

There have been numerous claims as to the powers of jade, only to be expected from a stone with such a long and illustrious history of use. Superstition born of ignorance often entwines and obscures, until all that can be seen is the superstition itself. This is not helpful; as in all matters one seeks truth through clouds of confusion.

One of the most persistent claims relates to this stone's beneficial effect on fertility. With jade, one cannot help feeling that this effect is more than purely physical. Jade pervades all levels. Any enhancement, though by no means all, may have its roots in spiritual and psychological areas, which are then transferred to the physical person.

Like icebergs, the greatest mass is hidden beneath the surface and only a small part is showing. People are like that. True, icebergs melt, but they melt into an ocean whose depths and power have yet to be fully understood. Jade may give the patience to understand – it may also give the time. (*See photograph page 53.*)

Jasper THE AMULET

This tightly-packed microcrystalline variety of quartz has also been known to exhibit a wide range of colours. Red jasper is usually indicative of the presence of haematite (*see page 48*), so straight away this should show that there can be a beneficial effect on the blood.

This 'amulet stone' has its healing roots in the history of half-myth and folklore. It is said to have once been used to protect the wearer against the turbulent negativities of other people. Negativities are like great upwellings in the oceans – full of power, surging from the depths, they will always be part of our lives. As part of society no one is a true island and we will, and should, always be in contact with other people. We will therefore always be prone to different types of infection and certainly prone to outside influences. We seek to influence others, sometimes from altruistic motives, sometimes for ulterior motives. People we know have probably wished for the powers of jasper to protect themselves from our folly. We are all only human.

In times before reason, jasper would be used by self-appointed holy men to dispel nightmares, demons and anything lurking in their own darkness which they couldn't understand. Do you think we have really changed? Perhaps the jasper has been swapped for something less tangible.

The wide spectrum of protection from this stone is mirrored in its physical attributes. It is known to aid against a whole host of minor ailments, but more specifically, because of the presence of haematite in red jasper, can allow a greater level of protection to the blood and therefore also to the liver. This may be how jasper's physical energy is transferred – via the blood. If the blood energy level is kept high and balanced, there may be less likelihood of minor physical infections and other ailments. The importance of haematite cannot be underestimated. It is present in many minerals and has a wide effect on their behaviour. Jasper is also said to be good for the bladder, but it is not known if this is true or not. (*See photograph page 54.*)

Jet   THE DEEP ONE

This dense black material is now a stone but once was not. It was once ancient driftwood that became engulfed in sea-floor muds and therefore could not degrade in the normal manner. It was then transformed into a coal-type substance called lignite, which is capable of burning but has a lower calorific value than coal. There are, therefore, very few extended deposits of jet, unlike stone and rock. The deposits tend to be a clumped series of individuals transformed through time, a different transformation than petrified wood.

In the past jet has been highly polished and used as a gemstone, the power potential of which is a complexity of Earth, air and water inextricably entwined around one another. Perhaps because of this, jet is one of the few materials known to aid chronic sleeplessness. Many minerals and crystals have the ability to relax, to arrange energies and stresses, yet jet, the ancient soporific, is capable of subduing the waves of wakefulness and carrying one to the depths. Like amber, there is a sense of timelessness about jet, of something once living under primitive skies, engaging the sense of curiosity in us all, engulfing us in the way jet itself was engulfed by the depths; we are carried away from surface turmoils. It could therefore, be helpful to a large number of people.

In the past, it is said, jet was used by those wishing to see into an unsure future. This in itself is bound to be an unsure art, even if feasible, but the ancient world was full of such things, and from it we are all born. To tell the future, either five or seven polished pieces of jet with symbols carved into them were apparently cast on the ground and, depending on the placement of each segment, signs could be read. (*See photograph page 54.*)

Kunzite   THE SUBLIME STONE

Kunzite is a form of the lithium mineral spodumene and is violet to pink in colour. It is transparent with a yellow/red to orange luminescence. Spodumene generally occurs as prismatic crystals, at times larger than 15 metres, or as rod structures composed of dense cryptocrystalline masses. As kunzite is pinkish in colour, other spodumenes can display a wide variety of shades and are an important source of lithium. Kunzite is quite rare, and good examples are often cut as precious stones.

Due to the lithium content (*see* lepidolite, *page 60*), kunzite is known to be beneficial for states of high emotional stress, excitability and especially addictions. Where willpower has been sapped, or is not as strong as it could be, kunzite can calm the internal chaos to allow the required strength to come forth. We all have this strength, yet sometimes it, too, becomes confused.

By calming excitable states, kunzite can then be used to help control any impulsiveness or compulsiveness. In certain cases, in combination with the increase in willpower, this self-control will lead to a healthy enhancement of personal self-esteem. This can then have a beneficial effect on all the negative states throughout the mind, body and spirit, strengthening the will and stabilising the emotions.

Life need not be filled with turmoil. Kunzite is much sought after because of its gentleness and subtlety. It is a soothing rather than imposing gemstone, with a calming effect, producing lower blood pressure and a healthy heart.

Kunzite is a stone for those who feel themselves lost in the frantic mania of this age of mankind, with temptations everywhere and life a constant rush. However, if you can step off the treadmill even for just a little while, you will see how much life is worth living. With kunzite you can have the will to rely on yourself, to make your own way through life and your own choices, and not be at the mercy of idle whims. (*See photograph page 72.*)

Kyanite   THE FAITHFUL STONE

Kyanite usually contains groups of light blue crystals of silicate material and is nearly always found in aluminium-rich rocks which have undergone high-pressure metamorphism.

The name 'faithful' is derived from the belief that kyanite is able to arouse faith, not only in oneself but also in one's partner, friends and relations. Most of all there can be faith in life, hope even when darkness seems at its most dense. We are all faced by such times and when the pressures seem at their heaviest we find the strength to continue. Kyanite is said to alleviate some of the anguish of this process, to make it less difficult, because it is a difficult time for all concerned. This also allows a person to become more faithful, inspiring loyalty and reliability. It is said that kyanite was once given to monarchs to make them good kings.

Some of the most important properties of this mineral relate to its physical potential, related to its psychological effects. By working on faith in oneself and dispelling those doubts of self-confidence that plague us all from time to time, kyanite is known to stimulate the creativity of certain individuals, mainly, of course, those who had little faith in themselves. This often shows itself as a greater vocal expression, and so has been utilised by those seeking a more extensive artistic range and by those who felt confused as soon as they opened their mouths. If we do not have faith in ourselves how can we expect others to have faith in us? We are not insignificant. Each of us is important in our own way, and together we are the society which strives for better things. The individual is important because at the real level of life it is mostly the individuals with foresight and courage who cause events that change the world we know. We all have this ability – kyanite helps us see.

From this there is a general expectation that kyanite is capable of aiding many disorders of the throat and upper airway tracts. Any physical effects in such areas are likely to be limited, however, yet with a growing confidence the mind and body together can work wonders. (*See photograph page 35.*)

Lapis lazuli THE BRIGHT NIGHT STONE

This is a crystalline lazurite and calcite rock with a rich blue colour that has entranced many observers into believing there are stars captured within it. For many centuries it has been much sought after, used as a gemstone and healer. Its beauty and power were legendary.

According to some people, in ancient times lapis lazuli was considered to hold incredible powers. Among the many claims, it was said to aid night sight and so was a favourite for soldiers, spies and lovers.

This gem can be a powerful arouser of the sixth sense, and was worn by ancient hunters as an amulet around the neck. It is also said to have been used by the holy men of the same ancient peoples to communicate with great spirits, but it is unknown how extensively this was practised.

These days, lapis lazuli is generally seen in a less dramatic light. It can produce a gentle and thorough relaxation throughout the mind, body and spirit, as a temporary remedy to anxiety and sudden stress. Much like descending night, lapis lazuli can blanket the turbulence with a fine veil to allow the senses to do what they do best – sense. In this day and age where there is so much sensory overload, such a power could prove quite useful. Perhaps it is this relaxation, this gradual 'fitting in' of all the pieces, which might produce a heightening of the hidden senses that allow a person to feel rather than see their way through the night. Night can bring tension from fear of the unknown. If this tension were to be relaxed, then surely more information could be gained from the senses.

If you have ever stood far away from the bright lights of the nearest town, far from headlights and noise, beneath a clear night sky alive with distant dancing starlight, you will have naturally felt your senses stretch to feel the limitless space above and around. Can you remember how it felt?

Although we know the scientific reasons for most things being the way they are, there is still a primitive awe to be felt deep down in oneself. This is a clearing of the mind, akin to the full effect of lapis lazuli. Standing at the centre of a network of nerve endings reaching out to anonymous night is an incredible feeling, and you just know there is more to life than we can see. The bright night stone clears away the darkness.

Lapis lazuli is also said to benefit the bone structure and a number of the deep glands. This may also be achieved through relaxation – a type of psychological T'ai-chi – placing oneself at one with the world on a more basic level than simply scientific understanding. (*See photograph page 71.*)

Lava   FOR SELF-PRESERVATION

Lava is the torrent of molten rock thrust up through underlying rock beds during volcanic action until it bursts through the ground, producing a crater. Most lava flows consist of the hardened igneous rock basalt, the lightest form of lava which when molten was more fluid and spread more widely than the others.

The four elements can be seen at work in a volcano, an ancient symbol of creation. As it erupts, smoke (air) rises from the crater, and earth and fire mix to create lava, which is liquid (water). As it touches water and cools, lava creates new land, so magical properties have long been ascribed to it.

In Hawaii, before European colonisation, lava rocks were used to build centres of religious and magical activities, some centres of healing. Of the several types of lava, two categories are useful, both known by Hawaiian names – *A'a* is chunky and rough, with projective or masculine energies; *Pahoe'hoe* or smooth lava, is receptive or feminine.

Lava is an energising substance, ruled by Mars and the element fire, and is believed to hold powers of protection. Utilise lava and feel its protective vibrations setting up sprays or fountains of glowing liquid lava which repel or send back consciously or unconsciously directed negativity to its originator. (*See photograph page 36.*)

Lepidolite   FOR CALMNESS

This is a mica mineral (*see page 64*) which is usually a pink to lilac colour, but on occasions may verge on the yellow. It occurs in some coarse-grained igneous rocks in association with other lithium minerals (*see kunzite, page 57*). It is the lithium content of this mineral which seems to concentrate its potential power; in medicine, some lithium compounds are known to have a calming effect.

For some time now this mineral has been known to have such a calming effect. It works mainly through the spirit, introducing a calmness which allays impulsion and desperation, preventing the chaos from overwhelming you, giving you time to assess your situation and to see the lack of reason for a course you were about to embark upon. The ability to reason is often misused, but if utilised properly will often lead to an enhanced enlightenment.

From here the calmness often radiates outwards, first of all to the mind and then to the body. While calming the mind, lepidolite has been known to help people give up bad habits. This is done by reducing the need. The physical effect is a mirror image of the psychological effect, and is achieved by calming the nervous system and strengthening the body so it feels it no longer requires anything more than it has.

Lepidolite is therefore capable of producing a complete peacefulness within a restless or agitated person. This can be used as an opportunity for further healing to take place. (*See photograph page 71.*)

Luxullianite   THE MOSAIC STONE

This is a rock formed by the alteration of granite by high-pressure high-temperature gaseous emissions from the late stages of a solidifying magma, whether the magma was a further volcanic intrusion or the original granite emplacement. (Magma is molten rock, including dissolved gases and crystals, found beneath the Earth's surface, and is usually indicative of volcanic activity. Granite itself comes from such a material.) With luxullianite there was an introduction of the metalloid element boron.

Luxullianite is recognised by its radiating clusters of black tourmaline crystals, quartz and reddened feldspar. A variety of this is called roche rock, and is a random distribution of black on white.

The 'mosaic stone' is held to be an aid to artistic talent by exercising the sub-conscious mind and freeing any restrictions found. To an artist there is nothing more frustrating than finding their energy 'blocked', whereas at the opposite extreme the artist may be a slave to inner inspiration. If either of these states persist for too long they can lead to unhealthy side effects. The 'mosaic stone' has the ability to even out the artistic temperament, to prevent frustrations and bouts of manic behaviour. This can lead to a more sustainable level of inspiration and understanding, and allow further exploration.

Inspiration need not be truly manic to succeed. Inspiration should have a sense of freedom not slavery about it. Inspiration is within us all, with its powerful waves and sirens calling. To free this would be freedom in a true sense, and should not be seen as attempting to 'capture' such freedom. Luxullianite is very rare, and expensive, so is not generally available from the usual rock stockists.

Malachite   THE FOREST STONE

With close connections to azurite (*see page 26*), and bornite (*see page 29*), malachite is also a copper mineral, found in the same type of environment as azurite. Valued as a gemstone, malachite is distinctive because of its banded emerald green appearance. Because of its copper content and colour, malachite is a highly energetic mineral.

Due to one of the natural forms in which malachite is found, it was once thought to enhance feminine curves. This is an old theory, based mainly on wishful thinking!

As with azurite, malachite is capable of regulating many of the major energy levels within a body. It often tends to be more physical than azurite. The balance of energies produced by malachite is subtly tipped towards the physical state. This has been found to be of use to people who require a lot of physical movement after initial concentration. Malachite will free the movement. Azurite and malachite are often found together, produced together, and in these cases they are best used together, one producing more psychological effects while the other tends to the physical. It is a good combination if it can be found.

In keeping with the effects of copper on the body's energy levels, malachite often aids sleep and dreaming (although it has a distinct crossover with azurite and even touches upon the powers of bornite). Malachite lends a peacefulness as a means of building up the 'biological battery' for increased physical energy levels during the waking hours. Taken holistically this is an important means of preparing the body because, as we are all aware, the body is part of the whole. It is unwise to attempt to prepare a part without consideration of the whole. During this restful time malachite can also aid, as an indirect effect, the blood vessels and blood flow, as well as those internal organs affected by adrenaline. It is a preparation of the physical being. (*See photograph page 17*.)

Marcasite THE BREATHER

This is a pale yellow sulphur-bearing mineral with close links to pyrite (*see page 75*). It is often found as huge aggregates in volcanic areas, but can also be a result of anoxic (lacking oxygen) sedimentary conditions. Jewellery fashioned from marcasite was once popular.

It was once thought this mineral could aid breathing disorders, but it is not much used these days. (*See photograph page 72*.)

Meteorite THE FAR STONE

A meteorite is defined as any extra-terrestrial solid mass reaching the Earth's surface. However, this would mainly consist of dust particles, the term 'meteorite' is more often restricted to:

♦ Aerolites – stones or stony materials which are composed mainly of silicate (quartz) minerals. This type is the most frequent entrant into our atmosphere.
♦ Siderolites – stony meteorites composed of iron and nickel as well as silicate minerals.
♦ Siderites – metal fragments composed almost completely of an iron-nickel combination, similar to the composition of the Earth's dense core.

Meteorites have been responsible for some cataclysmic events throughout history. Depending on mass and velocity, they can release a tremendous amount of energy on impact; the meteorites that survive do not have the required mass or velocity to cause an explosive impact. The Alvarez theory has shown evidence of an incredible energy release on impact of a large meteorite in connection with the dinosaur extinction 65 million years ago. Recent research has indicated that there are a number of large and fast meteorites passing close by our world.

Far from being the burnt-out stones that some would claim, meteorites have been known to give a sense of space, of timelessness, some would claim of eternity. Although specific benefits depend on the meteorite composition, those are the general benefits for which meteorites are best known.

Man has always been intrigued by time and increasingly is intrigued by the vastness of the universe. One more step for human curiosity. Touching upon time and space, inspired as some would claim by meteorites, would infer a release of the greatest mysteries the universe can hold. Whether a single mind could grasp the sheer immensity of this is doubtful, but there are claims that the potential of meteorites is an unexplored link which could lead to contact with other life forms.

It is not known whether this is possible, but common sense and statistics indicate that in the vastness of the universe, containing thousands of galaxies, with ours small indeed, the chances that the Earth is a solitary oasis of life amid a cold and dark void are slim. In other words, there is likely to be more than ourselves in the universe. The question is: do we want to be contacted?

This may seem far fetched, yet even 50 years ago the notion of landing on the moon was considered the type of science fiction to be relegated to the fringes of respectability. We can achieve what we want to achieve, and there is much out there in the great expanse of the universe to be discovered, much more to be understood. How can we, on our small planet on the edge of a small galaxy, hope to understand all there is to understand when we know so little of what is beyond the boundaries of our world? We are all human and so we try to understand as best we can. We are an ingenious species and use what tools we have.

Meteorite is a very expensive material; you will have to pay about £60 for a very small piece and you may find it is difficult to obtain.

Mica THE STRENGTHENER

Mica is a common stone and the general term for rock-forming minerals which split into paper-thin flexible sheets of translucent crystals. If a small residue from cooling magma becomes highly charged with water at low pressures it may solidify to produce very large crystals, among them mica, a rock of pegmatite formation. Mica crystals are hexagonal in form.

White or Muscovite mica is common potash mica, so called because it was once used in Russia as a substitute for glass. There is also biotite or black mica. The micas not only produce these large sheets but form the glittering specks in granite and similar rocks.

Mica is an energising stone, used for divination and protection, whose ruling planet is Mercury and whose element is air. Use it, therefore, for strengthening mental powers, and for eloquence, divination, study, self-improvement, communication, wisdom and travel.

Utilise it, too, for general protection. (*See photograph page 36.*)

Moldavite THE CHANGELING

Some have claimed that this material is the remnant of an aged meteorite, but this is not the case. Moldavite does have a meteoric link, however. It is, in fact, an impact glass similar to tektites (*see page 91*). When a meteorite of sufficient energy impacts upon the Earth's surface, the resulting release of energy will vaporise the meteorite and cause the material it has hit to melt. This melt material is specific to the area of contact and usually forms into a primitive glass. Meteorites that have survived impact are those with an energy below a critical threshold.

Moldavite is a melt glass specific to a single impact said to have struck approximately 15 million years ago. The material which is moldavite will have been changed beyond recognition from the parent materials.

Moldavite has a deep green colour, the shade usually associated with energetic healing. However, it is likely that much of the original impact energy will have dissipated during the latter stages of impact, and much will have gone into the alteration of the material into moldavite. It is probable that none of the meteorite properties will remain.

It is not easy to categorise materials such as moldavite because of their intense transformation, but as many impact glasses contain silicate (quartz) materials, the very general rule of quartz behaviour may be applicable. Indeed, moldavite is known to balance out the negative energies in a quartz-like manner. This, combined with the low level of energy within moldavite, ensures a gentleness and softness required by those who do not need a great deal of help, but who only want an occasional 'nudge' in the right direction. In spite of its appearance, moldavite is not a high-energy mineral, and is the sort of stone to be slipped between the pillows at night. (*See photograph page 72.*)

Moonstone THE GODDESS STONE

Moonstone is a gem composed of a silvery-blue alkali feldspar and has been compared to the moon at its full brightness. Folklore suggests that once upon a time a brave man in search of love reached up and cradled the moon in his hands. When his hands came down he carried with him pieces of moonstone as tears from the separation.

There is no doubt that the planet/satellite system of the Earth and the moon is unique in our solar system. By gravitational attraction the moon is responsible for the strength of the tides, and there is a connection with the cycles of the female body. The moon has been the subject of praise and romance since the birth of mankind, and wolves have sung to the moon. A recent theory indicates that the moon was not always situated where it is now, but was captured when it passed close to the Earth. Studies of the lunar surface would suggest this to be true.

Moonstone is so called not because it originated from the moon, but because of its physical and spiritual characteristics, especially its effects on women. Moonstone is reputed to ease the discomfort of many female ailments by relieving hormonal stress. However, its main potential is seen these days as being an aid to fertility, and in child bearing and afterwards to protect against the damage of depression. This is done mainly through an emotional balance attuned to the female mind and body, enhancing the female senses and wisdom, and spreading any discomfort outwards rather than inwards. Moonstone is said to enhance the feeling of romance inside oneself.

This can result in an openness to the world, a flowing like the tides, an acceptance of the feminine side rather than finding a way around it, which in some instances can cause internal conflict. The idea is not to be in conflict and therefore to weaken, but to enhance oneself through the strengths one possesses. The feminine outlook is a valuable attribute which moonstone can nurture, with a personal flexibility to suit the individual. Moonstone is a softer option than chrysocolla (*see page 34*); it is more subtle and 'user friendly', because of chrysocolla's close association with energetic copper. (*See photograph page 35.*)

Mother-of-pearl   THE MOLLIFIER

Mother-of-pearl is a gemstone of organic origin, the lustrous, opalescent interior of various marine or freshwater molluscs such as the oyster and mussel. These molluscs line the inner surface of their shells with nacre (mother-of-pearl), a form of the mineral calcite (calcium carbonate).

Since mother-of-pearl is the product of a living creature – the exterior skeleton or shell – it has been used in ritual jewellery throughout the ages, and sea shells were the medium of exchange in many parts of the world where metals were scarce or lacking, such as Polynesia.

Mother-of-pearl has a soothing and receptive energy; it is associated with water and the fifth element, Akasha, and its ruling planets are the moon and Neptune. Mystically it relates to the ocean, depth and movement, and is said to have protective powers. Place it on a newborn baby, for example, to protect it against the perils to come in life. Mother-of-pearl is also said to have powers related to wealth and money. (*See photograph page 18.*)

Obsidian   DARK VELVET

Obsidian is a volcanic glassy material, usually black, but other varieties can be brown or red, depending on the original magmatic composition. Obsidian is the result of a very rapid cooling of hot volcanic magma following eruption. Because of this, it is considered to have retained all the characteristic powers of a true fire stone, frozen into rock at a very swift rate.

Whereas moonstone (*see page 66*) and chrysocolla (*see page 34*) are considered to be feminine stones, obsidian is definitely the masculine side. Some say the male energies from obsidian are subtle; this must be because such people are not adventurers at heart. Obsidian is not one of the most subtle materials used in crystal healing, but each variety retains its own characteristics, its subtleties of character. For instance, silver-sheen obsidian is lighter and more friendly than the hypnotic depths of rainbow obsidian.

Indeed all obsidians can clear the heart of doubts, and if there is any adventurous spirit therein, obsidian will allow it through, to be felt, to be experienced, and perhaps to make the heart race with expectation. Obsidian will cause many a man to smile without knowing why he does so. A primitive surge. Perhaps it is this spirit reawakening within him. Like a waking giant it will want to yawn and stretch. It will need to express itself and do away with the thin veil we all surround ourselves with. The deep spirit within you will awaken and want to taste freedom. This may prove an overwhelming reaction. Such a spirit, verging on the barbarian must not, however, leave civilisation behind.

Crystal healing is about caring and helping. Materials such as obsidian may be used to free the masculine spirit from restrictions, but should not let it rampage out of control. We are not alone in this world, but for an adventurous spirit there are always barriers to reach beyond, new freedoms and understandings to be gained; there is never really any need to stop. There will always be space for an adventurous spirit.

If this is not enough, obsidian has more to show, more to give to he who wants it. The awakening of an adventurous spirit is merely the beginning, and before the end there may be a host of changes. This glassy stone from the heart of a volcano has the ability to benefit the loins and the stomach, to increase the metabolic rate and increase expectation. Obsidian can make the energy flow from you. Take a step forward to feel the draw of the life you once dreamt of. The dreams are still there, buried beneath crushing restrictions. Feel free, feel life and let the world know you are here.

This is not for the faint-hearted and is wasted upon the barren, as even mighty obsidian cannot create an energy that is not there in the first place. Before a fire can be built there must be fuel and a spark. The inner vision induced by obsidian is all that is needed to light the fire. (*See photograph page 54.*)

Onyx THE HEARTH STONE

This member of the broad chalcedony family (*see page 34*) consists of straight and parallel alternating coloured bands. It is related to agate (*see page 15*), with the main physical difference being that agate bands are always curved.

Whereas agate can be good for courage, onyx has the capability of aiding self-control. There is a subtle link between the two. Onyx and agate seem to be shades of one another. When dealing with the intricacies of personality each subtlety is an important difference. Each truth has many shades and means different things to different people.

As an indirect effect of self-control, onyx can produce a lessening of stress and stress-related conditions which may be caused by internal confusion. Onyx seems to be able to calm troubled waters and allow through a more essential 'you'. These may seem similar powers to those of a number of other minerals, but those same minerals tend to end here, whereas onyx, with its close links to agate, has the ability to nudge you towards courage. This allows you not merely to glimpse the world as it is and then perhaps return to what you're more used to, but to allow the 'real you' to stand up, showing – without fear of criticism – the differences you've always wished you had the courage to display. (*See photograph page 71.*)

Opal THE RAINBOW STONE

This unusual material can be classed as a gel, a mineral, a mineraloid (a non-crystalline hydrated mineral, held together in a discrete form, usually as a type of hard, dense gel containing individual mineral fragments), or a cryptocrystalline. Its chemical make-up indicates a variable amount of water, at times reaching an incredible nine per cent. This is due to the precipitation of opal from silicon-rich solutions at low temperatures.

Opal is called the 'rainbow stone' not only because it can occur in most colours, but also because precious opal can maintain a play of colours. One type of this opal is known as fire opal because of its colour.

The flashes of colour are said to stimulate the deep glands within the body. They are also said to exercise the retina and stimulate the optic nerve through to the reception site in the brain. The theory is that here the information will be transformed into a series of electrical impulses, and depending on the colours, hence the energy of the impulses, the opal can then effectively exercise certain parts of the brain.

The areas of the brain affected are not likely to vary greatly between individuals. However, with so many energy variations from different stones, so many synapse connection possibilities, it is not surprising that effects can vary. Generalities are few, but there does seem to be a heightening of brain activity from those areas affected, with the possibility of a quartz-like reaction dispelling negativity. This in itself opens many doors to personal growth and, depending on the energies from your particular opal (there is always a distinct element of chance with opal), there is likely to be a general psychological 'massage', a blowing away of the cobwebs.

At this stage there will be a clarification of the thought processes, a lightening of everyday life, allowing a strengthened link between the physical and spiritual self. The indirect effects of this are immense and must not be underestimated. However far this is taken is purely dependent upon the individual. Each opal tends to be unique in its individual energy-dispensing mechanisms. If you find an opal that is good for you keep hold of it, as you may not find another. Generally we each allow too many chances to pass us by. (*See photograph page 35.*)

Pele's tears   THE INVIGORATOR

Named after the Hawaiian goddess of volcanoes and fire, Pele's tears are rounded or tear-shaped smooth basaltic lava glass (*see* lava, *page 60*). They are rarely more than half an inch long. This glass is produced when a volcano erupts, or merely splutters, throwing out numerous small pieces of liquid lava which solidify during their flight.

Long filaments of lava are often attached to these tears in their original molten state. These are sometimes more than two metres long. When the lava solidifies, the filaments more often than not break off and can drift long distances upon the wind. Such filaments are known as Pele's hair.

Pele's tears, like obsidian (*see page 67*), are said to contain all the energies of a fire stone. Unlike obsidian, however, they do not have any gender connotations, nor are they as widely available. There are, however, a number of similarities between the two, due mainly to the energetic processes of production. Obsidian is obsidian, but will vary from area to area across the world because of the magmatic compo-

LCITE

LAPIS

RNELIAN

LEPIDOLITE

ESTITE

ONYX

RYSOCOLLA

PYRITES

RINE

SODALITE

AQUAMARINE

KUNZITE

AZURITE

MARCASITE

GOLD

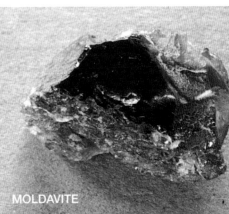

MOLDAVITE

HERKIER DIAMOND

SUNSTONE

sition, so it is no surprise to find at least some similarities with Pele's tears at some point. There are also a number of definite differences. Whereas obsidian is known to be deep and fiery, Pele's tears are very airy, with similarities mainly to silver-sheen obsidian.

Pele's tears, as the name 'invigorator' suggests, are reputed to be an excellent light 'pick-me-up', without the far-reaching consequences of obsidian. By allowing a more positive frame of mind, a greater clarity and freedom from self-doubt, this stone is able to reduce apathy, the twentieth-century malaise that allows a person to give away personal responsibility through default. To retain any figment of control over our own lives, we must not dispense with personal responsibility. Apathy, that self-imposed isolation, leads to a terrible waste of time. Pele's tears give the freedom to see. This is a freedom many people decline to use, however, perhaps because they no longer wish to see themselves.

In their gentle manner Pele's tears may therefore reduce inner chaos and frustration, reducing any stress and allowing an active individual to strive for and grasp new opportunities. They are a light breeze stirring the fallen leaves on a forest floor. Rather than a constant need, they are a 'leg-up', a brief aid to alleviate a temporary state of mind; as such they are not often used with any great success against entrenched states of mind.

Opportunities cannot be wasted, lest the mind and body become immune. Life is in a constant state of flux, and there must be movement if there is to be life. Pele's tears can help achieve this in their own gentle way by beginning the movement. The remainder, as always, is up to the individual. Deep down we all have the required strengths, yet sometimes our arms are not long enough to reach them.

Peridot THE SOOTHER

Sometimes called chrysolite, this dark green, translucent stone is volcanic in origin, and a form of quartz (*see page 77*). It is very similar (some say identical) to olivine, and the powers attributed apply to both.

Peridot possesses gentle, receptive energies. Its ruling element is earth, and it is associated with gold. To be at its most effective, it was once set in gold as an amulet. The ancient world believed this guarded against night terrors and illusions.

Peridot is said to have powers of protection, sleep, health and wealth.

Wear or carry it for general healing. It is said to promote healing of insect bites and to help in liver ailments. Cups or vessels made of peridot were said to have been used in healing because the medicine drunk from them was more effective.

Peridot calms the nervous system, soothing the nerves and dispelling negative emotions. Wear it to bed to help you sleep, and let it calm anger and attract love. These uses of peridot date back to Roman times, when peridot rings were worn to relieve depression.

Its dark green colour suggests its powers to attract wealth. (*See photograph page 53.*)

Petrified wood THE BALANCER

A microcrystalline quartz and a member of the chalcedony family (*see pages 77 and 34 respectively*), petrified wood is found mainly in the southwest of the United States. It is also known as fossilised wood. Millions of years ago trees were covered with mineral-rich water. The water slowly dissolved the wood and replaced it with various minerals, producing petrified wood. It is a grey-brown conglomerate of muted tones, and can contain light brown, yellow, red, pink and even blue to violet colours. The shape and structure of the wood are preserved in the stone.

As it is very earthy, it will help you to stay 'grounded' and balanced, bringing harmony within you so you can think and reason clearly.

It is said to be a general strengthener of the body, and is therefore useful for arthritis and the skeletal system. It helps the body combat the effects of environmental pollution, and because of its great antiquity is said to extend our life span and/or increase our enjoyment and evolution of our lives.

The American Indians used it in amulets as protection against accidents, injuries and injections because of its hardness and strange appearance. In earlier times it was thought to 'scare off' evil; now it is seen as setting up barriers of energy which deflect negativity.

It is thought to bring good luck, build up reserves of physical energy, help ease emotional and mental stress and encourage emotional security. (*See photograph page 53.*)

Pumice   THE BANISHER

Pumice is a volcanic product. If the gases which accompany an eruption perforate the lava with numerous holes, the lava hardens into pumice. Pumice has curious properties; it is light and rough to the touch, but floats on water.

Pumice is a substance with energising powers, whose ruling planet is Mercury and whose ruling element is air. It is said to have powers in protection, banishment and easing childbirth. At one time it was pressed into the hands of women during childbirth, to ease the passage of a new life into the world.

Use it if you have a problem you wish to banish – a damaging habit, negative emotion, physical ailment or unrequited love. Send the energy which is behind the problem into the pumice, visualising it as streams of thick, black smoke, then throw the pumice into the water – a lake, stream or ocean. As it hits the water it releases the problem, and the pumice, floating on the surface, is a symbol of and strengthens your ability to 'rise above' this and all negative conditions.

Use its power to absorb negativity for protection generally. (*See photograph page 18.*)

Pyrite   FOOL'S GOLD

More correctly called iron pyrite, this mineral has close links with marcasite (*see page 63*). Formed in a number of ways, pyrite is widespread throughout the world, but usually only in tiny flecks. The main pathways of formation are either by volcanism or underwater chemical reaction. Formation by these routes displays a lack of oxygen; they are termed 'reducing conditions', similar to the Earth's atmosphere prior to the introduction of oxygen.

When two pieces of pyrite are hit together they may sometimes cause sparks because of the iron they contain. This mineral is called 'fool's gold' because gold miners used to mistake it for gold; the name does not pertain to any personal use.

Pyrite is often formed at depth, and it affects the depths of a person. Pyrite is not difficult to come by and is very popular.

Willpower and the will are extremely important in crystal healing, as they are in everyday life. If there is little or no will, the person is likely to fall by the wayside, not by succumbing to temptation (which can sometimes be quite good), but by not having the drive and energy to succeed, to reach for better things. Without the will to succeed there is little chance of success in the more important aspects of life. Pyrite can aid this process. Happiness and contentment often come through achievement, no matter what the level of that achievement. Happiness and contentment are two of the greatest contributors to personal satisfaction. The will to succeed is an integral part of this, of human nature as a whole. The will is capable of transforming dreams into reality – and we all have dreams.

By strengthening the will pyrite often allows an emotional stability previously only the sure could afford. This can branch out into a confident and inspiring frame of mind (not necessarily completely positive), often allaying the doubts of those close to you, resulting in a greater harmony, a closer personal contact and understanding. Relations with other people are always important for a healthy personality. Success in whatever form you choose will be at your fingertips. All you have to do is reach that little bit further and grasp it fully with both hands.

The physical effects of pyrite are mainly those associated with greater flexibility and willpower within the mind and spirit. The digestion is the main beneficiary of a stable system, with less incidence of ulcers, sleeplessness and attack by the killer, stress. Because of pyrite's iron the blood is also known to benefit, but in many instances this may merely be seen as a natural progression of ensuring the body is in perfect condition.

Pyrite works from the depths. It may look a dramatic mineral, but its approach is less energetic than some, in spite of its iron content. Above all it is a harmoniser of the mind, body and spirit and all else between, which allows the strongest qualities to shine through with confidence and without fear. With its reputation for effectiveness, this is a favourite with many people, surpassed only by crystals of quartz. (*See photograph page 71.*)

$\mathcal{Q}$uartz (clear) THE UMBRELLA STONE

Pure quartz is crystalline silica. It is one of the most common rock-forming minerals, but must not be taken for granted because of this. As it is relatively hard and resistant to abrasion and environmental weathering, it is a common ingredient in many sands. This lasting quality is a clue to its power potential; where other minerals may weaken, quartz continues its protection regardless.

Rock crystals are natural, large quartz crystals, often prized. There are many types of quartz. *See also*: aventurine, hairstone, Herkimer diamond, rose quartz, rutilated quartz, smoky quartz; and the coloured forms of quartz: agate, amethyst, carnelian, cat's eye, chalcedony, citrine, jasper, onyx, peridot, petrified wood, sard, sardonyx and tiger's eye.

Clear quartz is known as the 'umbrella stone' not because of its shape, but because its potential seems to cover almost everything. Because of this quartz is a favourite stone for people's pockets, pendants and almost everywhere else, and has been for centuries. Certainly the varieties of quartz, including those above, probably contain the full spectrum of potential. They must all be seen as branches emanating from the stem of clear quartz.

Quartz deals with energy. In this it is no different from many other crystals and minerals, yet it is so successful and widespread because of the way it deals with energy. A powerful relaxant from the tensions imposed by deep negative energies, quartz strives to balance such energies in a more effective way for the individual. People often find their first use for quartz wherever concentration and relaxation is required, especially in meditation or yoga, where the body learns to flow with the spirit.

In a synchronised action only the powerful can display, quartz clears chaos from all levels, enhancing the 'oneness' between mind, body and spirit, elevating the whole, protecting and healing. Its effect on negativity is second to none. More than this, its actions can be so great as to be felt outside oneself, by other people. This, however, is likely to be a projection from yourself as you seek a higher plane of understanding and being. Such a plane may be reached by quartz lighting the path for your feet to tread. Naturally, we all seek the higher plane, to raise ourselves above the turmoil some people work to perpetuate, since it is in their interests to do so.

Quartz is a channeller not of possibilities, but of probabilities, and for this reason is able to transcend the limits of twentieth-century 'normality'. (*See photograph page 18.*)

Rhodochrosite   THE COURAGEOUS ONE

This banded red-pink rhombohedral (crystal system) manganese mineral forms in medium-temperature hydrothermal veins to produce granular or concretionary masses, or in stalactitic formations. (Concretions are mineral masses different in composition from the rock which surrounds them.) Rhodochrosite can be used as a manganese ore if the deposits are commercially viable, but is mainly used as a sought-after semi-precious stone.

This mineral is called the 'courageous one' because it is said that the banded redness helps to arouse a deep courage and passion. Working in a similar fashion to the colours of opal, rhodochrosite is a good example of 'colour therapy'. The courage and passion aroused are, as always, a means to an end and not the end in itself.

Rhodochrosite is often used by people who have suffered severe or extreme psychological trauma, or even a spiritual breakdown. Courage and passion in this instance are not blind; they are used to find faith in oneself, a special healing faith to rise above the threatening chaos. At times this may be a fight for survival.

This is called humanity. Humanity is in us all but has always been in short supply in the world at large. Rhodochrosite can enhance this humanity on a very personal level, allowing inner confidence to surface and break the chain reaction of struggle and suffering that swallows people whole every day somewhere in the world.

There are many types of love and many types of courage. The courage agate inspires is the courage to stand up for what you believe in with energy and conviction, not to be drowned or lost among a multitude of negativities, each reaching for the light and obscuring the personal positive aspects. The courage of rhodochrosite is the courage to be at peace, to reach the sublime, to float on a warm sea. Obviously these two are different and appeal to different sorts of people for different reasons. Because of the way the world is, or rather the people in it, agate tends to be more widely used because of its energy in achieving the aims of the individual; this in itself is mainly due to the complexities of quartz, haematite and other minerals.

Rhodochrosite is more of a quiet relative. Having few links with the energy of quartz or haematite, it is not in this stone's nature to inspire a person to take the world by storm, to right every wrong with a zeal verging on the brash. No, rhodochrosite is gentle and calming, peaceful and so enlightening, raising the person above the clamour of conflict they seek to avoid. Rhodochrosite relieves the addiction to stress, giving a relaxation that enables you not so much to cope with modern life, but once more to take your own life in your own hands and not feel so small in a huge world.

Physically, as a mirror image of this renewed psychological independence and gentle strength, there is likely to be felt a general vitalising of all life – a sort of excitement as you realise you have no need to struggle every day. Here the low energy of this red mineral can ensure a lasting enhancement of most physical signs instead of a more energetic but short-lived reaction. Rhodochrosite is courageous in its vision of peace. (*See photograph page 35.*)

Rhodonite THE THOUGHTFUL ONE

Rhodonite is linked to rhodochrosite (*see page 78*) – but not as closely as some people believe. Rhodonite is a deep pink to brown silicate and manganese mineral. It is not used as a manganese ore. Typical of a mineral metamorphosed from impure limestone, the colour is shot through with black veins of manganese oxide. This leads to a basic set of different powers than rhodochrosite, yet as with many minerals, there is usually some overlap, especially when the colours are similar and there are one or more constituents in common.

Rhodonite is called 'the thoughtful one' because it is said to help improve memory and encourage the spirit to search for the answers to those all-engrossing questions. The actual areas of the mind affected are likely to differ slightly between individuals because of differences in mineral colour and the amount of black manganese oxide. These other areas of potential are almost always likely to include a calming of anxieties by reducing the burden and impact of self-doubt. This may be seen as being connected to the principal powers of rhodochrosite – arousing a type of courage in oneself, by facing doubts and overcoming them. Where rhodochrosite can arouse pure philosophical courage, however, rhodonite allows a more realistically thoughtful approach, giving time to think problems through and find solutions specific to the individual.

Apart from the physical relief as you become more confident and less stressed, rhodonite is not known to have any direct physical benefits. Because of the wide-ranging powers of some more easily accessible stones, rhodonite remains a largely unrecognised gem of gentleness, an island haven amid a sea of turbulence. (*See photograph page 35.*)

Rose quartz THE LOVE STONE

As a branch of crystal quartz (*see page 77*), rose quartz is known to hold a powerful influence over those seeking crystal healing. A step further than the dispelling of negativity by crystal quartz, rose quartz can take you into the unforgettable realm of quiet love, sublime and pure, untarnished by the raggedness of modern life. By succumbing to love, rose quartz can effect in a person fundamental changes with far-reaching consequences. This is a stone for the born romantic. It is said that if a line of infinite distance was drawn, the two ends of the line would meet on the opposite side of the universe. The two extremes of love and hate are among the most powerful movers of human nature; they are so far apart yet so close. The power of rose quartz is in the energy it liberates, for love to overpower all that stands in its way.

The negativities mellowed by rose quartz are those specific to love – fear, jealousy, resentment, among others. It can also allay hidden guilt and anxieties, thereby smoothing the path for a purer under-standing, a compassion to be born within oneself, born not of agony and isolation, but of humanity. All too often with a quartz mineral the negativities are dwelt upon for too long, possibly because we all have too many of them to begin with. All too often the positive aspects of quartz are overshadowed. This is unlikely to happen with rose quartz because, with such a powerful and happy emotion as love, this itself is likely to place everything else in shadow.

From the birth of a true love, with all its innocence and purity, it is likely that there will be an easing of any sexual reservations or imbalance which have previously been a cause for concern. This is a major reason for use these days, yet what it comes down to is a deep relaxation. From inside out rose quartz relaxes the deep tensions we all suffer, allowing the energies to flow. Many people use rose quartz for meditative purposes. The secrets are not covered over or hidden deep, but can be exorcised, perhaps to be released within the general flow of energy, to be forgotten or forgiven. From this point it is a small step to the possibility of an increase in fertility, especially in men. Infertility in a significant number of men and women does not have a physical cause. Relaxation is the key to many problems, and within that relaxation rose quartz calmly exorcises the hidden tensions we may not even admit to.

More gentle than summer rain, rose quartz can help you achieve your dreams of emotional satisfaction. Surely this is worth contemplating? With so much dissatisfaction in the world it is good to feel the completeness of love. This is why rose quartz is so popular. Disenchanted in a technological world with impoverished personal contact, our inner selves yearn for true love to make us complete, to gently caress us. With all the temptations the world has to offer, love is ageless, love is superior, love is for us all. It is one of the great truths of humanity. (*See photograph page 53.*)

Ruby THE TRANQUIL

With close connections to sapphire (*see page 83*), ruby is the red gem variety of corundum, a mineral of aluminium. The colour of ruby is attributed to the presence of the metallic element chromium. For thousands of years rubies have been cherished, and not only for their beauty or as tokens of power and passion.

Much sought after, ruby is seen as having the ability to clear the mind of lingering vortices of turmoil, to find – as the name suggests –

tranquillity. This tranquillity is then a platform from which to improve the mind and body, spreading the warmth to dispel coldness.

The importance of ruby is that it can work where there has only been limited success with other stones. Limited success is usually a sign of either disbelief blocking the processes or of a deep-rooted turmoil intertwined with the fabric of one's thoughts. By inspiring tranquillity ruby has the potential to identify such disturbances and act as an overall tonic. The disbelief may be a sign of insecurity. Some people are just not susceptible to the powers of crystals and minerals, however, and if ruby fails to inspire them then all that can be suggested is that they keep on trying over a longer timescale, in an attempt to loosen the blockages holding them from a greater understanding. Generally, however, ruby can be of help to all but the most intransigent.

An opening up in turn aids many physical needs. As the mind becomes more willing to accept regrowth, opening its energies instead of imposing restrictions, the body will do likewise. This is most noticeable in tissue regeneration and the preservation of bodily activities. All too often, the body breaks down following a break in the spirit; tiredness, anxiety and fear are results of an inner conflict, manifesting themselves in time in physical disorganisation. If such stresses were relieved permanently, the physical body would not undergo any breakdown so readily. Once relieved it is much easier to protect against any further stresses of a similar nature. Ruby has this ability. (*See photograph page 17.*)

Rutilated quartz   THE REJUVENATOR

Clear or smoky quartz (*see pages 77 and 88 respectively*) with threads of titanium dioxide (gold or silver filaments) running through it, much rutilated quartz comes from Brazil. Varieties include hairstone (*see page 49*), needlestone, Venus hair and ulexite – angel's hair (*see page 96*).

It is a very powerful healer, said to be able to cut through mental and spiritual blockages. It enhances the life force, stimulating mental activity and preventing or easing depression. It is said to strengthen thought projections, transmute negativity and enhance communication to the higher self.

Use rutilated quartz to energise, rejuvenate and balance the system. Physically it is said to help tissue regeneration, by aiding the body to assimilate nutrients, helping the immune system to function more effectively and slowing down diseases of ageing. (*See photograph page 36.*)

Sapphire THE LOYAL GEM

Sapphire is the pure gem form of the mineral corundum, ruby the red gem variety (*see page 81*). The best known type of this gem is blue sapphire but other variations include green and yellow.

The beautiful form of sapphire makes it a more physical gem than ruby. This may be due to the higher energy colour of the former. Like ruby, sapphire has the fundamental ability to clear the mind in preparation for greater deeds, resulting in an emotional balance that is the basis for improvement and strength.

Sapphire is known to have a beneficial effect on the body, mainly through the glandular system, thereby achieving a balance specific to the individual. This benefits the digestive system, which aids the healing process by providing the required nutrients. Misused and often troubled, the digestive system is the only route of energy flow into the blood. If the digestive system fails to work properly or is given the wrong foods, then of course the body will weaken, followed by the mind and spirit. Physical sapphire allows the mind to balance through the body.

This is rather like a chain reaction: if the mind feels good, the body feels good; if the body feels good, the mind feels good, and so on. As the personal positive aspects begin to shine through, the world will prove to be an irresistible place of discovery where you can rely on your judgement, the clarity of which will be unclouded by turmoil or confusion.

The body is an incredible evolutionary machine which responds constantly to a fluid environment. As sapphire reacts through the glandular system, it will be able to keep pace with the changing environment and you will be able to give your best in any situation. This is good for dealing with the unexpected – and in today's world it is wise to be prepared. (*See photograph page 17*)

Sard   THE CONFIDENCE-GIVER

Sard is a reddish-yellow or brown variety of quartz (*see page 77*), related to carnelian.

Thought to be more effective for women than men, it is an energising stone whose powers relate to love, protection and courage. It is said to ease childbirth, and was given to women in labour to promote trouble-free birth.

Ruled by Mars and with its element fire, use sard for protection, to defeat negativity directed at you, and to promote courage. Courage is *knowing* that you can face any situation; use sard to create your self-confidence and the body's projection of personal power.

Sardonyx   THE ENERGISER

Sardonyx is a form of chalcedony (*see page 34*), layered with brown sard. Like sard, it is an energising stone, ruled by Mars and fire, and is said to have powers for protection, courage, marital happiness, eloquence, peace and luck.

Wear it or place it near the heart to relieve depression and despondency, and produce peace and joy. Use it, too, to end domestic strife and encourage communication between lovers or married couples.

Wear it to promote courage and fearlessness; in ancient Rome a figure of Hercules or Mars was engraved on the stone for this purpose.

At one time it was engraved with an eagle's head set in silver, platinum or gold, and worn to bring good luck. (*See photograph page 36.*)

Scheelite   THE TOUGH STONE

Scheelite is a tungsten ore, transparent to translucent, and displaying a wide variety of colours. The lustre of this material tends to be greasy. Scheelite can be found in crystals, in granular masses or massive aggregates, with only the best pyramidal crystals suitable for healing. In its natural state scheelite can be found in association with molybdenite, fluorite, wolframite or quartz (*see page 77*). Apart from their use in healing, the best crystals are sometimes used as precious stones.

Scheelite is said to have a long history of use throughout northern Europe. Apparently crystals used to be worn as defence against the cold. However, there is little evidence of its continued use these days, perhaps because it is very rare. You may have to search hard to find a shop which can obtain a piece for you.

Selenite (Gypsum) THE YOUTHFUL STONE

Selenite is a form of the widely distributed mineral gypsum. Selenite is found as colourless and transparent monoclinic crystals, or on occasions in large crystalline masses. Like gypsum, selenite can be found in evaporite deposits (those formed by evaporation of former seas or salt-water lakes).

Selenite is called 'the youthful stone' or 'the rejuvenator' because of its potential for stripping away the accumulated burdens of age. This is not the same as the longevity potential of jade. People tend to wear time heavily; it is a sad reflection upon most societies that even though time is precious, people often waste a lot of it, and abuse the remainder. People become heavy with the dust of time, with pent-up emotions, barely recognisable frustrations and hidden fears, all of which conspire to lessen the worth of an individual from the inside out. With the heaviness of time and the struggles of everyday life, people lose their direction in life, and their dreams and hopes.

With the will for it to work selenite has the potential to remedy this bending of the spirit, this cluttering of the mind and exhaustion of the body. Older people often wish for their youth once more, because they wasted so much of it.

Selenite is capable of working deep, ridding a person of the heaviness of time which ties them down, by blowing away the accumulated dust and allowing free movement, thus halting the progressive and barely noticeable run-down of life. Of course, not everyone is affected by age in the same way, but there are times when we all feel the years heavy on us; this tends to creep up little by little. Time is so valuable to our physical selves, but not so much to our spiritual selves, which are as ageless as love.

By working through the levels, the potential of pure selenite crystals can have the effect of rejuvenating, of quite literally 'lifting time'. In this way selenite may be linked with amber (*see page 20*), although they work towards different ends. Whereas amber lifts time from the mysteries of past lives, selenite lifts time from this life. Further than we can see even the stars are measured in time, yet beyond the expanding universe where we can barely comprehend, where there is nothing, is there an eternity of nothing? Does time cease to exist there?

With selenite making you feel younger there is also likely to be a relative increase in your sexuality. Care should be taken. The eyes can sparkle, the smile can return, and on occasion there can be a tightening of the skin, especially around the face, where many emotions are carried. There will be a youthful air about you as years of stress are relieved. This must be the best tonic of all. (*See photograph page 18.*)

Serpentine THE GUARDIAN

Serpentine is a metamorphic rock. It is attractively variegated in colour, and can combine green, yellow, black, red, brown or be mottled, with white streaks. It is translucent to opaque with a slight lustre, and although it belongs to the monoclinic system, it does not produce crystals, being massive or fibrous or flaky.

With its ruling planet Saturn and its ruling element fire, this is an energising gemstone with powers for protection and lactation. Nursing women wear serpentine around the neck to regulate their milk supply. Serpentine seals were carried in ancient Assyria so the gods and goddesses would send double blessings.

Its main use is in guarding against poisonous creatures – snakes, spiders, bees or scorpions. Creatures in their natural environment will bite or sting to defend themselves or their territory, so carry or wear serpentine whenever you are camping, walking or hiking, and in contact with nature. It may help to prevent misfortune. (*See photograph page 18.*)

Silver THE SHINING STONE

In its mineral form silver is distributed in limited amounts in the upper areas of more extensive ore deposits. Larger amounts of silver minerals, like numerous others, may be deposited from hydrothermal activity. Pure silver may be found in some deposits.

Silver has a long history. Like bronze and gold, it is a traditional metal for jewellery making. Precious and alive, it has caught man's imagination – and sense of greed – since the dawn of time. Yet silver was not always used for necklaces, brooches and bracelets simply because of its supposed financial worth. There have always been other reasons for wearing silver.

Today is no different from yesterday in that there are, have been and will always be people with too much guilt and fear and similar potentially destructive blockages within the mind and spirit. We do what we must to survive, yet it leaves us with scars running deep, with barely hidden disturbed dreams and anxieties that approach the surface in disguised form, at times to wreak havoc. Such blockages reduce the effective flow of positive energies, and serve only to distort the true person with a bitterness and frustration too much for others to bear. There will be a good person beneath it all, screaming to be heard, to be free, and yet the guilt and fear have wound themselves so well around the spirit that they have effectively become the new person.

Silver has been known to alleviate this. It has the ability to free the real you, breaking the chains you have felt for so long and allowing you to feel the sun on your face. Silver can allow the strength to change. Such crumbling of restrictions may take some time, depending on the individual, but the change will come from within and will last as long as you have the strength for it to last.

In the same way, silver has been known to break down those blockages affecting physical behaviour. Sometimes there may be so much pent-up emotion that a person cannot even speak properly. Silver can offer a sense of freedom. Many people who wear silver are more talkative than before they were in contact with the metal.

Silver was once considered to protect the wearer against curses and demons of the night – perhaps this is why werewolves can be killed with a silver bullet. Thus silver is also said to protect against fear – not only fear of the unknown, but fear of failure. Many a brave person has been held back by fear of failure. It is the ability to overcome this fear which is the difference between the brave and the unbrave. There have always been many reasons for wearing silver. (*See photograph page 36.*)

Smoky quartz THE CONJUROR

This is a pale yellow to deep brown member of the quartz family (*see page 77*), renowned for its ability to enhance dreams, at times to a very high degree. Once used extensively for this purpose, these days smoky quartz is used more for its general relaxation abilities. The two are, of course, linked, as it is through thorough relaxation, by an expulsion of negativity, that dreams, sparkling like stars in the night, may be spun and woven with a conscious effort, bringing forth the subconscious in a deep welling of energy.

Once you are relaxed there may be a number of paths you can tread. As always, it is completely up to you – you are in control. The crystal does not control you; it is merely a method of achieving your aims.

For a deep examination or manipulation of stress, as in all quartz, an even deeper relaxation is a prime requirement. This is where smoky quartz has an advantage over many other types in its family. Quartz generally balances negativities for a more healthy frame of thought and being, enhancing relaxation as the stresses are released; smoky quartz is said actively to raise the personality following a stripping away of the negative aspects. From this point one may not be able to resist the temptation to explore. Perhaps because of this sense of relaxation, smoky quartz is known to aid sexuality.

Like a deep massage, smoky quartz can open doors to the borders between the limited consciousness and the limitless subconscious, where we might sail like a ship on an endless ocean. Such relaxation!

Many people tend to find new qualities within the different members of the quartz family. It's almost as if the crystals retain many of their mysteries until the person is ready to learn them. Quartz is the most popular and more widely examined of all the crystals, yet the depths remaining are uncharted because they are personal depths. The unknown qualities of smoky quartz are, if anything, more extensive, simply because for too long it has remained in the shade of clear quartz in many people's thoughts. Why this should be so is not known. Clear quartz maintains a wide potential, yet smoky quartz is different in numerous ways and should not be ignored. Its dream-enhancing abilities are second to none and surpass even clear quartz in this area. Dreams are important as the mind expands. Above all the mind requires expansion into new areas. (*See photograph page 54.*)

Sodalite THE CLEAR ONE

The name 'the clear one' is not related to this mineral's physical attributes, because sodalite is bright blue, white or grey, at times with green tints. It is a feldspathoid mineral (akin to feldspar), occurring in compact masses.

The name relates to the effect sodalite can have on a person. Unlike many other minerals, sodalite is known initially to work through the body, progressing to the mind and spirit. Most other minerals show a reverse pattern of action.

Sodalite's main mode of action is often through the lymphatic system, strengthening the body against infection and stress. The heart beats more surely, thus stabilising any fluctuations in the metabolic rate. More than this, the colour differences of this mineral can have an increasing importance, spreading any benefits out in a series of tangents. Once more, the individual must test several varieties and choose the most beneficial type for themselves.

Progressing through the physical body this new stability and energy can then have psychological and spiritual benefits. This is where the name 'clear one' comes from. The mind is earthed by the physical stability and inspires communication with all other levels. The spirit is cleared of all confusion, flowing into the mind on waves of creativity to inspire a gentle calmness from a sure mind and body, as well as a rested spirit. (*See photograph page 71.*)

Sugalite THE SOUL STONE

Sugalite is a translucent, elegant magenta-coloured gemstone composed of sodium, potassium and iron minerals. It was discovered in 1944 in south-east Japan and named after the petrologist who found it. In its natural state it is both massive and compact, with lower grades displaying a cloudy and mottled appearance, or with alternating bands of dark and light. Sugalite is highly prized for jewellery.

Sugalite is said to increase the strength and foresight of the spirit – it works deeply. The radial expansion of the spirit is sure to affect every aspect of a person's life. Sugalite is known to increase awareness, sensitivity and courage. It may indeed initiate a transformation, allowing the true self to shine through with a strength of will to overcome life's obstacles.

The spirit is a strange entity seen from our view of reality. In fact it is part of us, requiring nourishment in the form of intellectual stimulation. It requires exercise in the form of adventure – stretching out and discovering, perhaps touching upon others' lives at a level of common subconsciousness mainly experienced during the deepest dreams. There are claims that sugalite can help the spirit reach a common subconsciousness – and perhaps beyond – because, really, the human spirit knows no bounds.

The spirit is as much a part of us as our bodies – the hidden part, that huge mass of the iceberg unseen beneath the surface. Barely understood and often neglected, it is the part of us that can lift us from inherent barbarism and chaos. In the right hands sugalite is said to aid this journey to civilisation. One day we will outgrow the world.

Physically, as a direct result of any spiritual enhancement, sugalite is said to work through the glandular system, protecting the body, freeing spiritual strength for physical tasks. Consequently it is partly known for its beneficial physical effects, mainly because such effects are more noticeable than deep spiritual enhancement.

Sugalite is for the adventurous, for those who know they have more to give the world, the ambitious and sincere. This gemstone may take you some time to get used to it, but as always, the more effort on your part the greater the reward. Try hard – pour all your self into it and be sure that great things are yet to be. (*See photograph page 17.*)

Sunstone   THE WARM STONE

In no way connected with gold, sunstone is an aventurine feldspar (*see page 25*), usually translucent, which gives a reddish glow. The glow is due to tiny plate inclusions of haematite (*see page 48*), lying in parallel.

The energy of haematite in sunstone is said to warm the mind and spirit, and to purify all the body. Because of the colour of this stone and its mode of action, it is important to be able to see the stone and not hide it away in a pocket and hope it works. Gaze deep into the heart of sunstone to feel waves of warmth and comfort flow from the spirit, where too often there is only the coldness of isolation. In this way you may reach a higher consciousness. This is often seen as the effect of the aventurine component. Physically, the encouraged warmth is said to give added protection to the body, especially the blood, because of the included haematite.

Used correctly, it is claimed that sunstone can engulf the mind, body and spirit in its red glow and its state of independence, and can enhance a state of 'higher self', so it feels as if there is no gravity. This experience is said to be short-lived, but worth the concentration. Who knows what might be perfected with practice? (*See photograph page 72.*)

Tektites FOR INNER SPACE (*SEE* MOLDAVITE)

Tektites are created by high-energy meteorites (*see page 63*) impacting on the Earth's surface. (They are usually large and fast moving, the smaller and slower meteorites usually do not have sufficient energy.) As a result of the impact and resulting energy expense the meteorite is instantly vaporised. The energy released can, under specific circum-stances, cause a mix-melt of the rocks within the immediate area of impact, allowing any volatile constituents to escape. This mix-melt tends to be glassy in nature. If the energy release is sufficient, small pieces of the mix-melt will be thrown into the atmosphere where they attain a spherical shape. Most tektites are dark and small. The most famous of these are the tektites from 65 million years ago, which are said to mark the extinction of the dinosaurs.

Each group of tektites is unique to the area of impact. Moldavite, for example (*see page 65*), which is green, comes from one specific area in eastern Europe. Tektites are said to give a sense of space – not outer space but inner. They are said to be able to relieve claustrophobia and agoraphobia, depending on the energy level. (*See photograph page 17.*)

TIGER'S EYE

Tiger's eye   THE CHAMELEON STONE

This is a gem variety of quartz (*see page 77*), which can exist in a number of distinct colours. The most popular of these is gold tiger's eye. The chatoyancy (changeable lustre) of the golden variety is due to a usually extensive penetration of the quartz by crocidolite fibres, a type of asbestos. No, don't worry, the crocidolite is firmly fixed into the quartz and can be handled with safety. Gold tiger's eye has been in use for a very long time and completely overshadows other varieties, such as red or blue. The play of light along the bands of gold can at times be hypnotic.

With the remnants of a fire stone and the typical behaviour of a quartz, this gem is for the brave. It often inspires courage and strong willpower, certainly an immense will to survive, to strive for greater success. This is the basis of gold tiger's eye – striving for success. This is helped by allowing a person a clear perception of what is taking place, and the ability to think ahead. For the ambitious this is essential. The ambitious, at times, take leaps where others take steps. Tiger's eye seems to enhance this natural enthusiasm.

Rather than lending a sense of co-operation, there can appear a sense of competition in those who are this way at heart. With tiger's eye there is no complete harmony as there is with some other minerals, and so it should not be used by those wishing for a quiet and peaceful life. It is true that tiger's eye inspires, but in a way which is uncommon among other quartz minerals, and it may have an adverse effect on the unwary. Among other effects there may, in fact, be too much confidence, and this must be guarded against in some instances. Yet the potential of tiger's eye is such that it seems to know a person's limits and rushes to this point, only to stop before it's too late. This may suit the brave, but is not for the unwary. Quartz tends to dispel negativities, but even negativities have their place at times and sometimes it may be reasonable to be cautious.

At times courage and foolhardiness go hand in hand, so this is a classic example of teaching oneself self-control, relying on oneself rather than on the potential of the gem. Do not abandon responsibility for your own life and actions. Tiger's eye leads to an excitement, a euphoria of cascading joy; you will cast all caution to the wind as you rush forward with open arms to feel a vibrant world. Dramatic? If you let it be.

Physically, tiger's eye is known to aid the digestion. As the body's means of gaining energy this is a logical step into the physical side, and may be helped by the correct type of diet. Toxins are invariably introduced into the body from the air we breathe, the water we drink and the food we eat. If the body is unable to expel these materials it will store them. The storage of such toxins may give rise to sluggishness, among a host of other physical side-effects which can negate even the potential of tiger's eye. It may therefore be of benefit to look at your diet and lifestyle and find ways to improve them, to aid yourself and the power potential of the gem. (*See photograph page 54.*)

Topaz THE EXTRAVAGANT ONE

Sometimes known as 'the abundant stone', topaz is an orthorhombic silicate mineral often found as huge crystals, which are much sought after. Possible colours range from yellow to violet, or it may even be colourless, and it can be found in some metamorphic or igneous rocks as a result of high-temperature, high-pressure gaseous reactions. Such energy expense in the creation of this mineral ensures a high retained potential.

Topaz is known as 'the extravagant one' because of the extravagance of its potential. Partially, perhaps, because of its wide range of possible colours, it is said to be able to do almost anything – 'the abundant stone'. It is said to be the cure for all twentieth-century ailments. While some of this may be the exaggeration of eagerness, topaz is known to have an extensive range of powers. It can awaken the imagination, and when this happens anything is possible.

The wave of inspiration flowing from this crystal may at times be overwhelming. It is a joy to hold. It is enough to waken all the senses into a warm day where everything is indeed possible. With its sense of peaceful creativity pervading throughout all levels, unlike tiger's eye, topaz is a co-operative and happy stone that fits in well with the calm and unhurried higher consciousness – a complementary gem, sure to disentangle the best qualities of any person.

Physically, the same sense of peaceful creativity can give you the feeling of a 'new' self, enhanced health as the inspiration carries you higher, where self-expression becomes increasingly important. This 'new' self is likely to involve most of the inner body and can be especially effective in tissue regeneration.

Tired? Feeling stressed because of a mental block? Run down? Topaz may be what you're looking for. For those seeking a new direction in life, topaz inspires inner vision to see beyond social conditioning and let happiness flow. (*See photograph page 53.*)

Tourmaline   THE RISING STONE

Known also as 'the Aquarian' or 'Aquarius rising', tourmaline is not a single mineral but a group of complex borosilicates (salts) whose chemical composition is a variable factor when assessing its potential. Tourmaline can nevertheless occur as prismatic crystals or groups of crystals composed of parallel or radiating individuals.

This mineral is common in metamorphic and igneous rocks. In pegmatite, a coarse-grained igneous rock representing a volatile, rich, late stage in a magma crystallisation, tourmaline may be found in huge crystals, due in part to pegmatite's slowness in cooling.

Tourmaline is a stone which has gained a great deal of prominence over the last decade from those requiring a combination of protection, comprehension, and the quartz-like dispelling of negativity. In fact, tourmaline has a far greater potential than this.

Because of the wide variation in its chemical composition, crystals may have a wide display of colours. This in turn may offer a full spectrum of powers people can find useful and convenient.

Throughout our lives society can unwittingly urge us into an insensitive approach to others, the world at large and life in general – unfortunate and unflattering, as basic humanity is often ignored. This also leads to inner conflict because deep down we know it is wrong to 'harden' ourselves to the ways of the world. This only spreads the conflict.

Tourmaline can alleviate this condition of isolation and return us to the humanity we all need. There is no need to struggle through life.

Tourmaline may help by allowing an increased comprehension of the world around us and our lives, our interactions. This leads to a renewed sensitivity, not only to all around us, but also to ourselves, as too often we undervalue our own lives and achievements.

Comprehension and sensitivity revoke fear and confusion. In this way, tourmaline is said to aid some psychological disorders, calming confusion and reinstating self-worth. Without self-respect there will be no striving, and striving for improvement is a great part of human nature. To be lost from this is a very lonely experience.

Tourmaline allows natural changes to take place, disturbing only the stagnation of an imagination tired from struggle. The results, however, are *your* results – your imagination, your will, your self. Tourmaline, as with every other crystal, mineral and gem, is a tool for you to gain the best results. The effort is all yours.

It's easy to see why tourmaline enjoys widespread popularity. People ravaged by the negative rigours of society seek a place to belong and a self which is worth calling a self. (*See photograph page 17.*)

Turquoise   THE ENVIRONMENTALLY FRIENDLY STONE

This is a triclinic mineral containing copper and aluminium. Because of the copper this mineral usually occurs in light blue or green microcrystalline formations and is produced by the transformation of aluminium-rich rocks in arid climates. For centuries turquoise has been seen as a valuable ornamental stone.

Turquoise is one of the master healers. The energy of the contained copper is particularly strong. As with all minerals containing copper, there is an effect on the energy levels within a body and beyond. Some of the claims made for turquoise may be more extravagant than for topaz, 'the extravagant stone', but no research has been conducted to determine the limits of this potential, if indeed there are any.

Probably because of the copper content, turquoise is known to aid the absorption of other minerals and nutrients into the body, usually via the blood. This is typical of the effects of an enhancement in the physical energy levels. With this there is always some degree of protection as the body's physical defences are at their most energetic.

It is claimed that turquoise can protect against all environmental pollutants, including background radiation. This is a powerful claim and must be considered very carefully.

Different environmental pollutants work in the body in different ways and it would be extremely difficult to guard against them all, although it would be possible to protect against some. Background radiation (not including the many man-made chemically-active radionuclides, which can be the most dangerous) may be a different matter. Radiation damage is caused by a transference of energy. Copper can control the energy balance within a body, with the possibility of negating any further transference and preventing damage. This would be an immense benefit, but more research is required before it can be assessed. It may, however, just work.

Increasingly, turquoise is being used to bring back an appreciation of natural things, of nature as a whole. This is seen as an extension of the mineral's protective abilities against pollutants. By inspiring a love of nature, sources of pollution will no longer be tolerated. So often we forget to consider the natural world, or consider it lightly.

As with many copper-containing minerals, there are mirror-image effects between the mind and body. With the physical absorption of minerals and nutrients to stabilise an enhanced energy level, the mind is likely to experience a lessening of any stress, manifesting itself in renewed abilities of friendship and reliability; the mind will open up with a strength and vitality emerging from a higher energy equilibrium. This higher state of being will be beneficial to all aspects of life and is likely to continue beyond what can be expressed by a few simple words. At times, communication may be so restricted. What is required is a 'feeling'; turquoise helps the individual to 'feel' their way to a more fitting life, without the distractions of modern living. (*See photograph page 53*.)

Ulexite ANGEL'S HAIR

This is a triclinic mineral containing boron, a metalloid element; it is found as light, spongy masses of white, silky, hair-like fibres. It is formed by solution precipitation during high levels of evaporation in lakes of arid regions. (*See also* rutilated quartz, *page 82*.)

Ulexite was once thought to enhance spiritual connections and psychic abilities, but is not used much these days. (*See photograph page 18*.)

Variscite THE PROTECTOR

This phosphate and aluminium mineral has a white-green or blue-green colour, depending on the energy of the material, and a greenish luminescence. It is dull and translucent, occurring in massive, crusty and reinform aggregates with orthorhombic structures. Similar to the mineral wavellite, variscite can be rare and used as a precious stone.

Variscite is an unusual mineral in the world of healing. It is said to protect the unborn child. Although there is no firm evidence for this, it is a widespread belief that its strong protective influence can safeguard those generations to come. As we seek eternity through our children, we have a responsibility to ensure their safety.

Variscite may indeed be able to protect the unborn child because it is also known to be a soothing healer in its own right, ensuring a physical and psychological stability. This in turn may be transferred to the unborn child, because anything that is good for the mother is likely to be good for the baby. In any age, women are sensitive to the well-being of their babies and recently the use of variscite has increased. (*See photograph page 53.*)

Zircon THE WISE ONE

This is a silicate mineral and an important source of the rare metals zirconium, hafnium and thorium. Zircon can be found in many acidic igneous rocks as well as in their metamorphic derivatives. Zircon can also be used as a gemstone, usually if it does not contain thorium.

Zircon's main use is against insomnia, usually by releasing stress and allowing relaxation. This weakens the heaviness and depression suffered by many insomniacs. Zircon is known to work through the subconscious, which in turn relates to spiritual well-being. In this way the mineral is said to balance the personality, not by introducing new aspects but by allowing what has been hidden to come forth.

Often this will continue on a spiritual tangent, but many have experienced a greater psychological benefit stemming from an untroubled outlook. This carries with it its own strengths and wisdom, the basis for the name 'wise one'. Zircon is often seen as a type of sedative linked to alleviating insomnia. It may also have some glandular effects as a physical means of almost forcing the body to rest. (*See photo page 36.*)

CHAPTER FOUR

Birthstones

*T*HE subject of birthstones is not straightforward. For a start, there seems to be a general confusion over which stones apply to specific signs. This lack of consensus has come about mainly because there are different stones applicable to different times of a sign. The stones should reflect a person's character and, depending on factors such as time of birth, the correct stone can be found and worn, if required, to lessen weaknesses and increase strengths.

Below are a number of general birthstones. Within your sign there may be others, depending on your character – and who you listen to!

Aquarius 21 JANUARY – 19 FEBRUARY

Amethyst

Blue sapphire

Pisces 20 FEBRUARY – 20 MARCH

Amethyst

Jasper

Aquamarine

Tourmaline

Aries 21 MARCH – 20 APRIL

Bloodstone

Lapis lazuli

Diamond

White sapphire

Taurus 21 APRIL – 21 MAY

Agate

Sapphire

Emerald

Topaz

Gemini 22 MAY – 21 JUNE

Agate   Moonstone
Green tourmaline

Cancer 22 JUNE – 22 JULY

Emerald   Ruby
Onyx   Turquoise

Leo 23 JULY – 23 AUGUST

Amber   Onyx
Carnelian   Peridot

Virgo 24 AUGUST – 23 SEPTEMBER

Carnelian   Peridot
Jasper   Rose quartz

Libra 24 SEPTEMBER – 23 OCTOBER

Alexandrite   Tourmaline
Opal

Scorpio 24 OCTOBER – 22 NOVEMBER

Citrine   Ruby
Garnet   Topaz

Sagittarius 23 NOVEMBER – 21 DECEMBER

Agate   Malachite
Amethyst   Turquoise

Capricorn 22 DECEMBER – 20 JANUARY

Garnet   Ruby

CHAPTER FIVE

Massage

◆

CRYSTALS and minerals are frequently used in some types of massage. What is required is a cut and polished specimen with a well-rounded side to prevent any physical damage. Large crystals and pieces of mineral are usually best. It is possible to obtain a cut crystal specifically for this purpose.

Warm the material in your hands before putting it on the other person's body. Work slowly, gently at first then with increasing strength, but never too hard to cause any discomfort. As the crystal warms and the movements over the body become more fluid, there is likely to be a subtle transference of energy to the patient, allowing a powerful relaxation from deep within. An initial application of a light oil may be beneficial.

Depending on the crystal, the masseur or masseuse, and the patient, different effects may be observed, but relaxation will always be deep and lasting. Keep the movements slow and sure, with the mind flowing through to the hands and to the warmth of the crystal. Feel the crystal wipe away tensions, feel it work deep to promote unification and harmony between mind, body and spirit. Giving and receiving such massage is a pleasurable experience, transcending barriers, which will remain with both people for a long time. The enveloping peace is sublime.

Ancient and perfectly natural, crystal healing may be the only therapy to unify the three parts of a person.

CHAPTER SIX

Meditation

*F*OR longer than may be imagined, crystals have been used as a natural focus for meditative energies. Essentially meditation is concerned with reaching deep into oneself, past the chaos and the stress which plague many people. Then the real self may be touched, may be recognised and elevated. This often results in the emergence of an inner harmony. Through this state of peacefulness, relaxation and clarity, one will see the world in a new light.

Many crystals are the perfect vehicle to induce and enhance a meditative state. This is the natural progression to the more general use of a crystal's energies. It is a step beyond simply having and holding the crystal.

It is obvious that different people will prefer different crystals or minerals. We are all different. We all have different deep-down stresses affecting our outer lives. You must choose the material you are most comfortable with – *your* crystal, *your* mineral, *your* stone. The most popular crystals by far are quartz, but with a growing number of people utilising the deep energies of obsidian or the light touch of amber. The emphasis here is on comfort. The one *you* feel most comfortable with will usually be the one to reach deepest within you.

To use crystals, minerals and precious stones for meditative purposes you must first prepare yourself in your usual manner for meditation. Each individual has their own individual method, but the result is the same – to reduce stress and prepare to touch the inner self. All else must be blocked out. You must focus. The crystal will help you focus.

Sit quietly and place the crystal at eye level in front of you, preferably with pure unadulterated sunlight upon its surfaces. The reflected energy may then pulse deep within your mind. With no distractions, you can concentrate on the crystal, feeling the energies flow out of and into you. Feel the crystal smoothing out the turbulence within mind, body and spirit, touching upon the inner flow of life, even upon timelessness. Once the turbulence has been sufficiently smoothed, the mind will entwine with the spirit and enter into a meditative state.

For a more active or swifter form of meditation the crystal may be held within open hands. Sit with your hands resting in your lap. Concentrate on the crystal in the same manner as before, but whereas in the previous example time is of little importance, here you may feel the crystal, feel its warmth and energy and how it delves deep to smooth out the turmoil all the faster. Because the crystal is being held its energies will be stronger and so will work more deeply than before, to enhance a deeper state of tranquillity from the union of mind and spirit.

Time is important. We tend not to make full use of it and wonder why it flies past so quickly. Sitting with your mineral in your hands, look at it and feel it so the energies both from the atomic structure and the colour are fully absorbed. The effect of these energies will always be greater if you are fully relaxed, as there will be fewer barriers against which to flow. Take as much time as you wish. It is important to allow the energies to penetrate deep. This is not an instant occurrence.

There will come a point of deepest conscious relaxation when you know you have pushed beyond the stress and turmoil holding you back. This is what the crystal helps you to do. With the crystal in your hands simply close your eyes and slip into the meditative state.

The latter may only usually be achieved after the former has been mastered. It may take some patience, yet the effect once it occurs should be like a lifting of the soul – such a peaceful effect. Once this is achieved there are likely to be few barriers to struggle against and you may apply all your hidden talents to attain a higher existence within the realm of things that are, not merely those we can see.

Crystals, minerals and precious stones have the ability to allow you to meditate more deeply and more successfully. The subtle energies of crystals achieve most when in contact with the other subtle energies of the mind.

The choice of suitable minerals will depend not only on the individual and on individual needs, but also on the type of meditation engaged in. Different meditation styles employ different methods; some seek to relax completely, some to get rid of stress and so relax. The end result is the same. For the more active forms of meditation the more active minerals, such as some of the copper minerals, might prove a suitable aid.

Generally, the quartz family is the most popular – clear quartz, amethyst, rutilated quartz, smoky quartz, rose quartz, citrine, Herkimer diamond. They are often beneficial for relieving stress and so enhancing relaxation and peace of mind, leading to further enhancements. As a potentially powerful combination the crystal ametrine, which is a natural cross between amethyst and citrine, is becoming much sought after.

The initial stress release encouraged by quartz is only the beginning. You may stay with a quartz for a greater attainment of peacefulness, but there are no hard and fast rules saying you *must* stay with the same crystal. Some people stay with the same crystal for many years because it holds a special comfort for them, as the energies reach deeper than any other. Some people will change crystals after they have achieved the initial mellowing of internal chaos. They require energies of a different direction for their individual needs.

It is therefore not possible to say that one crystal will lead to, say, spiritual growth in everyone. Crystal energies overlap greatly, and everyone is different. Indeed, not everyone will be affected by a crystal or a mineral.

Epilogue

❖

SPIRITUAL growth, or any other state, is unlikely to be enhanced straight away. By a holistic approach, the internal chaos in us all must first be dealt with, so we can examine ourselves in the clear light of truth and be free to venture in any direction we wish. This is the real potential of utilising the energies of crystals, minerals and precious stones.

Patience as always is important – that and the will to succeed. We are an ingenious people and can do anything if we really want to. Anyone who states the opposite is restricting themselves, and attempting to pass the restrictions on to you to justify their own lack of achievement. Before we reach for a higher understanding, however, we must first understand ourselves – crystal healing makes this possible. With crystal healing we may clear away the internal restrictions holding us back. With crystal healing we may glimpse a greater life and with our own will reach for that greater life, to feel ourselves awash with warmth and pure tranquillity.

This is the beginning of true greatness.